YOU CAN HAVE A

Happier Family

Other good Regal reading on this subject:
  Communication: Key to Your Marriage,
    Norm Wright.
  Good Times for Your Family,
    Wayne E. Rickerson.
  Look for the Wonder,
    Frieda Barkman.
  Sex Is a Parent Affair,
    Letha Scanzoni.
  You Can't Begin Too Soon,
    Wesley Haystead.

YOU CAN HAVE A Happier Family

G/L REGAL BOOKS FAMILY LIFE LIBRARY

A Division of G/L Publications
Glendale, California, U.S.A.

Norm Wakefield

Scripture quotations, unless otherwise noted,
are from the *New American Standard Bible.*
© The Lockman Foundation, 1971. Used by permission.
Other Bible versions include:
The Living Bible, Paraphrased (*TLB*)
Wheaton: Tyndale House, Publishers, © 1971.
Used by permission.
Berkeley Version in Modern English. (Grand Rapids:
Zondervan Publishing House, © 1959). Used by permission.
New International Version, New Testament. Copyright © 1973
by New York Bible Society International. Used by permission.

© Copyright 1977 by G/L Publications
All rights reserved
Printed in U.S.A.

Published by Regal Books Family Life Division,
G/L Publications
Glendale, California 91209. U.S.A.

Library of Congress Catalog No. 76-24320
ISBN 0-8307-0403-5

This book flows from my experience with some
of the special people in my life—
My parents, Francis and Edith Wakefield,
who guided my childhood experiences,
oftimes to their frustration.
My wife, Winnie, and our five children,
Amy, Joel, Jill, Jody and Annette,
who are teaching me
many valuable lessons about myself.
To these loved ones I dedicate this book.

Contents

A study guide for individual or group study is available for this book.

Foreword

With so many books already published on family life and child rearing, why add to the supply? Because I helped Norm Wakefield in the early going with this one, I can think of at least three good reasons:

1. *This book comes out of Norm's own life.* He writes out of the crucible of experience, not the vacuum of theory. Always positive, always constructive, Norm is still always the realist. He knows what it's like to be parent-on-the-spot. When he mentions Winnie and Amy and Joel and Jill and Jody and Annette, he is talking about real people who share his roof, eat at his table and tie up his bathroom.

2. *This book comes out of Norm's solid scriptural understanding.* He looks at parenting through the eyes of the biblical husband committed to loving his wife and not provoking his kids to climb the wall. But while Norm's philosophy is biblical, it is always applicable to life today. He doesn't agree with all the modern theories, but he doesn't discount the ideas that make sense. The reason is simple. Ideas that make sense usually jibe with the Bible. We have a very sensible God.

3. *This book comes out of Norm's organized disciplined mind.* Practically all his life Norm has been dedicated to helping others learn. He has been a professor

at Talbot Theological Seminary. He has taught in churches, at retreats, conferences and seminars. He is now in a full-time commitment to helping families be happier and more effective. His teaching is marked with practicality, specifics and student involvement. So is this book.

Of course Norm covers the "basics": developing positive discipline, taking time to build good relationships, using solid communication techniques. But he also goes into areas that aren't always covered in books on parenting: how and why you help your children learn, and how to read to your children. (Yes, there is more to reading to a child than pronouncing the words and turning the pages.)

Especially useful are the last two chapters—on values. These days there is a lot of theory on values, but there is little the typical parent can really understand or use right now in his or her own family. Norm's chapters on communicating your life-style and building Christian character offer practical help. Norm is edifying, but he still has empathy for today's overworked, overcommitted and often overwhelmed parent.

It doesn't matter where you are on the parenting scale. If you're just starting out, with kids in diapers or the sandbox, Norm's ideas can give you a solid foundation to build on. If you're well into the struggle, here is your survival kit to help you analyze where you're coming up a bit short and what you can do about it.

As Norm says of his own family, they are all growing, changing, becoming persons. So is yours. Accept that. Accept the frustrations. Accept your God-given role. Take time for the joys. You can have a happier family!

Fritz Ridenour

Introduction

Four Basic Family Goals for Christian Parents

I can still see her sitting there with tears in her eyes, relating to me the tragic account of a mother-daughter relationship that had gone sour. Their inability to accept each other had led the daughter to experiment with dangerous practices which scarred her psychologically and left the mother drained emotionally. Now, facing up to the situation, the mother sought counsel on how to correct the problems and rebuild the damaged relationship.

Thankfully all of my counseling memories are not of heartbreaking disappointments. I remember conversing with a radiant mother and her three teenage daughters. The deep roots of love were evident. The oldest daughter said to me, "Mother is my closest friend. I share things with her I wouldn't tell to my best girlfriend." What a delight to sense the rich dividends received from the positive, strong caring spirit built between this mother and her daughter.

What caused the difference? Why are some parents adequate parents who enjoy their children while others know only bitterness and sorrow?

Obviously, many factors come to bear upon the parent-child relationship. Circumstances beyond human control often enter in. Peer-group influences frequently place pressure on young people. And, ultimately each child exercises his own will—some stubbornly resistant, others graciously compliant.

Having acknowledged that circumstances vary and that each child responds as an individual I still hold to the following basic premise: *As a rule children become what the parents allow them to become*.

Usually well-adjusted children are the products of parents who provide a balanced diet of security, love, friendship, respect and discipline. These children are well-adjusted because their parents attempted to use constructive methods and resources to guide the development of their children. Faulty children are often the result of faulty parenting.

I say this for at least three reasons: (1) I believe this view is supported by research in the psychology of parent-child relationships; (2) I have observed these principles at work over several years of ministry to children and adults; (3) I observe the principles repeatedly in the Word of God.

Most newly-marrieds believe their marriage will work well. Most new parents believe they will be good parents. They are convinced they are special . . . for them things will be successful and happy. This feeling is probably rooted in the romantic complex ingrained in our culture that is expressed in the familiar: "They were married and lived happily ever after."

But "happily ever after" doesn't happen on its own. Instead, a happy Christian home is the product of mutual commitment of both husband and wife to realistic goals that both are willing to work at diligently.

What goals are important for Christian parents? I feel there are four basic goals for building a healthy family. These goals are what this book is all about.

BASIC FAMILY GOAL 1
To Develop Attitudes of Consistency and Self-discipline

At the heart of the thriving Christian family are a father and mother who recognize the importance of living out a well-rounded Christian life-style day in and day out. By well-rounded I mean that they want to be self-disciplined people who consistently communicate —by the things they do and say—the high priority they put on Christian values. They are well aware that their lives are models for their children and they care about providing dependable Christlike leadership based on biblical principles.

But Christian parents soon discover that in spite of their sincere desire to be self-disciplined, consistent examples of Christianity in action *it doesn't happen automatically.* In fact, the key word in the goal is "develop." Parents are in-process people, constantly called on to meet changing needs, with every day providing new situations, new challenges, and new opportunities for learning. For help in developing attitudes of consistency and self-discipline in your family, look at chapters 1-3 of this book:

Chapter 1 Choosing a Christian Life-Style

Chapter 2 Planning for Positive Discipline

Chapter 3 Discipline—from a Plan to a Process

BASIC FAMILY GOAL 2
To Develop an Atmosphere of Love and Unity

The thriving Christian home is permeated with a spirit of love and caring that builds family unity. That is easy to say, but the complex mixtures of feelings and the wide variety of situations in a family make an "atmosphere of love and unity" seem remote (even impossible) at times.

How can you make the difficult, unhappy child know he is accepted and loved? How can you encourage love between brothers and sisters who constantly feel threatened and often hostile toward each other? How do you effectively communicate love messages across a generation gap? How can you encourage unity when everyone in your family is an independent, strong personality who is concentrating on himself?

Love and unity, like other characteristics of the healthy Christian family, are the result of specific things parents decide to work at and do. Chapters 4 and 5 are designed to give parents practical suggestions for developing an atmosphere of love and unity in the family:

Chapter 4 How to Build a Good Relationship with Your Child

Chapter 5 How to Communicate with Your Child

BASIC FAMILY GOAL 3
To Provide Opportunities to Grow, Discover, Create

Children develop best in a climate that encourages their curiosity and creativity. This means taking time to

listen to questions and to answer . . . taking time to fee'
wonder instead of impatience when a young one asks his
umpteenth question of the hour and wants to know,
"Why do birds have wings?"

It also means giving children freedom to explore,
dream and imagine. They come up with wonderful fun
ideas. Recently, I cut down a tree that was too close to
our house. The pile of branches on the ground was just
part of the job to me—something to clean up. But as I
came around the corner of the house the children shout-
ed, "Daddy, look at our fort!" They had made themselves a great place to play with what I thought was a
useless pile of branches.

Helping children grow, discover and create also demands that we teach them responsibility. (The branches
had to be cleaned up later!) There is a proper balance
between freedom to explore and responsibility for action. As parents we are constantly challenged with keeping these opposing factors in a positive, creative tension
with parent and child both having opportunities to discover, create and develop new ideas. For helpful suggestions on growth, discovery and creativity in the family,
see chapters 6 and 7:

Chapter 6 How to Help Your Child Learn
Chapter 7 How to Read to Your Child

BASIC FAMILY GOAL 4
To Discover and Work Toward God's Will and Purpose for Our Family

How do you think your children see you? Frustrated,
often discouraged, involved in a treadmill of activities
that seem to have no real purpose? Or do your children
sense in you a certain stability and happiness that communicates: "Come on, I know the way . . . it's good . . .
let's all go God's way together"?

15

Christian parents who take God's Word seriously discover that Scripture does give definite purpose and direction for family life. The Bible spells out biblical principles and Christian values as well as giving specific instructions to parents, husbands, wives and children, defining their individual roles and responsibilities in the family. God's directions all add up to a way of family living that respects and glorifies God and at the same time makes life better for everyone in the family.

Chapters 8 and 9 deal with key issues involved in discovering God's will for families:

Chapter 8 How to Communicate a Life-Style
(Values)
Chapter 9 How to Build Christian Character

THE PURPOSE OF THIS BOOK

This book is written to help you discover how these four basic goals can encourage and enrich healthy family life at your house. Each goal is closely related to practical factors that I believe are involved in becoming a successful Christian parent. I share my discoveries and my convictions out of real life experiences as a Christian husband, father and educator. I write about the questions and problems (as well as the joys and satisfactions) that I have experienced with my own family. The illustrations are from everyday life at our house or from home situations that I know well.

Five active, noisy, challenging children make up the Wakefield flock. Winnie, my wife, and I find that each of our children has enriched our lives and challenged us to grow. At the time I am writing this Amy as a thirteen-year-old is rapidly shedding the image of childhood. At twelve years of age Joel seems to possess all of the energy which I lack! Knowing how to channel his abundant energy in constructive channels has been one of our big challenges. Ten-year-old Jill says that she is like her mother, a warm, friendly person. Jody, six years, is a very outgoing person, and her cheerful spirit attracts others. Annette, our five-year-old, has challenged us in a different way. Since her speech development has been slow she has taught us how meaningful each new step of growth really is.

There you have us—the Wakefields. But we are described here in only the most sketchy fashion. And today's description won't fit what we will be tomorrow. We are all growing, changing, becoming persons. All I know is, that for me, my family is the greatest.

Norm Wakefield

Basic Family Goal 1

To Develop Attitudes of Consistency and Self-discipline

1 Choosing a Christian Life-Style

As you read this chapter, you will discover . . .
- four key questions every parent must be able to answer
- why personal example is so important in child-rearing
- how husband and wife can stay in tune with each other
- why parents must be a child's friends as well as his parents
- why dad has to lead (not "lord it over") the household

Choosing a Christian Life-Style

How do you live out a well-rounded Christian life-style in the midst of marriage and child-rearing? It's not easy. Being married and involved in raising five children has provided me with a constant flow of challenges. My overall goal is to provide consistent Christlike leadership for my family. The challenges are the nitty-gritty, everyday questions about how to put my goal into action.

Do Your Children Know You Love God?

For example, Winnie and I have a deep desire for our children to love and read the Word of God early in their lives. Fine. But what does this say to us?

Already, the children have demonstrated to me that their interest in the Word of God is best stimulated by my own excitement and joy with the Scriptures. If I am truly interested and enthusiastic when I share a Bible passage or story with them they mirror my feelings.

God knew this principle centuries ago. In Deuteronomy chapter 6, He challenges parents to love Him with their total being—heart, soul, mind and strength. He stresses that this love must be written on the heart and lived out in the daily life-style, morning, noon and night; " . . . when you sit in your house and when you walk by the way and when you lie down and when you rise up."

When my wife and I read this Scripture portion, we have to ask ourselves some soul-searching questions. Can our children see a deep commitment to God in our lives? Can they tell that we love Him? How brightly does the light of Jesus Christ shine in our lives? What areas of our lives need to be renewed by the Spirit of God? Bad temper? Patience? Disinterest in others? Neglect of Bible study? Ability to show caring love for one another?

The counsel given in Deuteronomy chapter 6 challenges parents not only to maintain a deep devotion to God, but also to strive to communicate this love to their children in everyday ways. In daily conversation mothers and fathers have good opportunities to share the reality of their relationship to a loving Father. And by their attitudes and actions parents *can* be living examples of the Christian life!

Children can also sense their parents' love for Christ through visual expressions in the home. In fact,

Deuteronomy 6:9 indicates that the importance of the Word of God should be visualized before a child's eyes. Winnie and I believe that a home can tastefully express Christian values through *carefully chosen* plaques, decoupaged verses and pictures. I sometimes ask parents, "If I were to come into your home what would tell me that the people who live in this house love Jesus Christ?"

Do Your Children Know You Love Each Other?

How a dad and mother treat each other says much to a child. A good husband-wife relationship is a key factor in consistent Christlike leadership in the home. Children need to see dad and mother being considerate of each other, enjoying each other, being loving and thoughtful. By contrast, when parents frequently argue, criticize each other and seldom show love and thoughtfulness, they create a climate where it is difficult, if not impossible, to communicate meaningfully with their children about God and His love.

Because a comfortable, loving, husband-wife relationship is such an important part of developing a Christian family life-style, it is vital that both husband and wife be keenly aware of each other and how things are between them.

Can Children Come Between a Husband and Wife?

Do you sometimes feel your children are a wedge that drives you apart? Are you so busy meeting the needs and demands of the children that you have little time for each other?

Some parents have discovered the value of periodically spending a day or two together—apart from the children—as a way of strengthening their relationship. It's healthy for a marriage—and for the family as well—that

22

husband and wife have opportunities to concentrate on each other, talk together, enjoy the fun of planning and doing just what they want to do for a day or two.

Recently, Winnie and I arranged with a dependable woman to stay with the children while we spent several days together at a Christian conference ground in the mountains. We enjoyed sharing the inspiration of the conference as well as the hours we had alone together. Our time away together deepened our bonds of intimacy and strengthened our husband-wife relationship.

Much of our love is expressed in the way we communicate. For this reason mom and dad need to maintain a daily pattern of effective communication between themselves. Many couples have found it is helpful to reserve some time together for relaxation and sharing the day's events, mutual interests and plans for the future. Some have found that taking a walk together provides a quiet peaceful time when they can enjoy each other's presence. Others schedule a night each week to go somewhere together. In every case, parents must find effective ways to keep building their relationship *with one another.*

Children measure parents' love for each other through the emotional tone of their communication. You can't fool children. They know if their parents love each other by the way they talk, by the sound of their voices, the look on their faces.

In his book, *Communication: Key to Your Marriage*, H. Norman Wright points out that Christian couples should make their home a safe place in which to communicate: "Strive to establish and maintain a permissive atmosphere in your home. In a permissive atmosphere both marriage partners are free to share openly and honestly what they feel, think and believe. Each family member is allowed to speak the truth in love."[1]

Do Your Children Know You Love Them?

A consistent Christian family life-style intimately involves the children and their feelings. Family goals and plans mean little unless children and parents feel good about each other. Can your children depend on you? Are they sure of your love no matter what?

The Christian parent's example of Christlike leadership begins with a vital relationship to the Lord, progresses to a loving relationship with his/her spouse and reaches out to a close meaningful relationship with each child. A child's parents should be among his best friends; his closest counselors; people he can trust and go to with his questions, joys and problems. However, when parents usually judge harshly, ridicule or berate a child, the youngster is not likely to feel comfortable with them or to grow close to them.

I have often asked parents to write out their response to the following statement: "My children know that I love them because ... " Many parents reply, "They know I love them because I have told them so." I believe effective love must be received as well as sent. What do I mean? Simply this. I may tell my child again and again that I love him, but unless he sees it visualized in actions and deeds that he feels good about, he has reason to doubt me. This is why we read in 1 John 3:18: "Let us stop just *saying* we love people; let us *really* love them, and *show it* by our *actions*" (*TLB*).

This deep caring love of which I am speaking is an essential ingredient for your child's healthy development. Without it, self-esteem has a tough time taking root in your child's life. If you don't communicate your love and respect to your child he has a difficult time learning to respect himself. Sadly enough, I have met many Christian parents who genuinely care about their children but cannot communicate it effectively. The result? The parents cannot understand why their children have low self-esteem.

Dorothy Briggs, author of *Your Child's Self-Esteem*, gives parents invaluable advice when she says: "Nurturing love is tender caring—valuing a child just because he exists. It comes when you see your youngster as special and dear—*even though you may not approve of all that he does.*"[2]

Briggs observes that many subtle parental attitudes such as criticism, overprotection, lack of respect, excessive demands and comparisons communicate a lack of love, though the parent may care a great deal.

Does Your Family See Father as the Leader?

According to God's plan for the family, the father's role as a consistent leader and loving guide is vitally important. Scripture underscores this in Ephesians 5:23 and 6:4: "For the husband is the head of the wife," and, "Fathers, do not provoke your children to anger; but bring them up in the discipline and instruction of the Lord." As a husband and father I have discovered that in our family's everyday life things go better when I take seriously the responsibility for loving leadership and *lead.*

As a teacher, I frequently read the writings of anthropologists, sociologists and psychologists as I prepare to teach. It is interesting to note how often their studies mention the importance of male leadership and authority in the development of a healthy family climate. Today's research confirms God's plan for family life!

American culture is democratically oriented so we tend to think mostly in terms of a democratic Christian home. But this concept is foreign to Scripture. Practically speaking, a husband and wife cannot function as a democracy. Let me illustrate what I mean:

A situation demanding decision develops. I vote *for* . . . my wife votes *against.* Deadlock! God in His infinite wisdom designed the Christian family around certain fundamental concepts that avoid deadlock situations. One of these concepts is that *the Christian husband and father must rise to the challenge of leadership with love.*

Here's a real life illustration from the Wakefield family. Recently we bought a house. We had asked the Lord to provide one with a large yard for our five children. In the process of hunting we located a lovely house with many excellent features but the yard was small. By this time we were somewhat weary of house searching and we began to think about the many lovely qualities of the house all the while minimizing the limitations of the small yard.

We took a family vote and the vote was 5 to 1 in favor of buying this house. (The baby was too young to vote.) I was the lone person who felt uneasy about the decision. I had been impressed with the prayer of Jabez when he asked, "Wilt Thou grant me a true blessing and extend my boundaries" (1 Chron. 4:10, *Berkeley*), and I felt keenly that I should trust God for the original request that our family had made and prayed for.

When I shared my feelings with the family my wife quickly said, "If you feel that way then we will trust God with you for a home with a larger yard." In a very short time God honored our prayers of faith and we did find a home with a very generous yard that really meets the need of our active, growing family.

The point is this: The husband/father must assume the responsibility for loving leadership of the family under Christ if a truly Christian life-style is to develop. When the father fails to lead, he weakens the entire family structure and the family cannot become all that

God intended for it to be. God's Word counsels: "Where there is no leadership the people fall" (Prov. 11:14, *Berkeley*). This concept holds true for the family as well as the nation.

PARENTS' PLAN FOR ACTION

A consistent Christian life-style takes work and above all it takes planning. You need to set goals, choose priorities, make plans and then work day by day seeing what happens.

Use the following exercise to evaluate where you as an individual are *right now*. Then go on to the "What We Want to Do" section and set some specific goals for improvement. If possible work together with your spouse on these activities.

Where We Are Now

Check appropriate column.   WEAK   FAIR   GOOD

1. My personal relationship with the Lord.
2. My ability to communicate my love for Christ to family members.
3. The quality of my relationship with my spouse.
4. My ability to communicate with my spouse.
5. My ability to communicate with my children.
6. My ability to communicate love to my family members.
7. (For fathers) The fulfillment of my role as a loving leader for my family.

27

8. (For mothers) My willingness to let my husband lead.   WEAK   FAIR   GOOD

What We Want to Do

Prayerfully decide on the *one* most needy area above in which you want to improve. Attempt to identify *specific, achievable* actions which will lead you to improvement. Suppose you choose number 3 above as your project. You might list such activities as:

1. Set aside 20-30 minutes daily to spend alone with my spouse.
2. Plan with my spouse how we can use the 20-30 minutes in the most constructive way.
3. Prepare a special treat for my spouse at least once a week.
4. Read *Communication: Key to Your Marriage*, by H. Norman Wright (Regal Books).

Footnotes

1. H. Norman Wright, *Communication: Key to Your Marriage* (Glendale: Regal Books, 1974), pp. 160, 161.
2. Dorothy Corkville Briggs, *Your Child's Self-Esteem* (New York: Doubleday and Co., 1970), p. 61.

Basic Family Goal 1

To Develop Attitudes of Consistency and Self-discipline

2 Planning for Positive Discipline

As you read this chapter, you will discover . . .
- a good definition for discipline
- the positive as well as the negative dimensions of discipline
- that discipline is much more than punishment
- Scripture's unfailing model for discipline
- good discipline depends on a good relationship between parent and child
- the characteristics of a sound plan for discipline

Planning for Positive Discipline

Few areas of family life are as emotion-filled as the subject of discipline. Few stimulate such diverse views. Few areas generate such strong reactions and few are based upon such a limited understanding of Scripture!

A well-educated, earnest Christian vented his frustration as he said to me, "What am I to do? My parents taught me one way; my education has taught me another way! My wife feels we should handle the children gently; I think we have to use a no-nonsense approach." He was genuinely frustrated because he was uncertain about this crucial area of child-rearing.

In my own experience there was a day when I realized that I was disciplining my children as my parents had disciplined me. I was assuming that this was the "Christian way." At that time I had completed Bible school and had graduated from a Christian college. Yet, I had never thought through the Scripture basis for discipline. I suspect that countless numbers of Christian parents are in the same situation.

In this chapter I want to focus on those pieces of the discipline design that have completed the picture for me. I do not believe that the problem of discipline can be settled with one or two simplistic words of counsel. Those who approach the subject on a "to spank or not to spank" approach have a very limited view of what discipline involves. It is a richer, more profound aspect of the parent-child relationship.

When discipline is properly utilized, it gives the family stability. Family members understand the rules of family life. They feel more secure because discipline provides the acceptable, safe limits in which a person can function freely. Positive discipline is a fence that gives children the security of knowing how far they can go.

If you are beginning a family, one of the important tasks you will ever have will be to think through your understanding of discipline. Though you may not be aware of it, it is essential that you realize how heavily you have been conditioned by the way your parents disciplined you. Deep within, you may hold resentment toward a particular form of discipline—spanking for example. Perhaps your parents used spanking in an unwise or incorrect manner and you say, "I'll never discipline *my* child *that* way." Or, you may respond in the totally opposite fashion. "If it was good enough for my parents it's good enough for me!"

Either approach can be defeating because neither asks "What is the right way?" You cannot develop a sound approach to discipline by defending or attacking.

Reporting on a study of how a child's character development occurs, Peck and Havighurst in their book, *The Psychology of Character Development*, note that love and discipline are two essential ingredients. Since discipline is such an influential aspect in the character development of a child, it is crucial that parents discipline in a proper way. I think of discipline in terms of a design. I believe that each piece of the design is essential to a healthy Christian view of discipline.

Just What Is Discipline?

Part of the problem in building a design for discipline is that frequently an adequate definition is lacking. Somewhere in the past I discovered a definition that has much meaning for me: Discipline is guiding, supervising, and educating a child's choices.

This definition helps me put discipline into a proper perspective. It helps me see that there is a positive as well as a negative dimension of discipline. Too often discipline is thought of as only punishment or penalties.

Many parents fail to realize that whenever they help their child make a decision they are disciplining him. Suppose, for example, that Jill, our ten-year-old, comes to me with this problem: "Daddy, Cindy wants me to spend the night with her, but if I do I won't be able to go to the parade with you tomorrow. What shall I do?"

Jill and I discuss how she can make a wise decision. No thought of punishment is even involved yet I am guiding and educating Jill in the way to make a wise choice. I am helping her become self-disciplined.

32

Most of us need to expand our discipline horizons. We must spot the many situations in which we can help our child make wise choices. Then we will have more concern for a preventive rather than a solely corrective approach to discipline. Corrective measures are necessary at times, but my wife and I enjoy showing our appreciation to our children for the wise decisions they make, instead of only correcting unwise decisions.

When we view discipline from a positive perspective our attitude changes. We then capitalize on the positive occasions to teach. We realize that we have the privilege and opportunity to prepare our children for the lifetime of decision situations they will encounter. Seeing discipline in this light helps parents avoid merely reacting to the problems that are a part of each day. Instead we act deliberately to instill basic principles of action, conduct, and decision-making into our child's life.

Needed: The "Right" Discipline Model

One reason many parents are indecisive about discipline is they don't know whom to believe! One child psychologist, who is for democracy in the family, says: "Since democracy implies equality, parents can no longer assume the role of the authority. Authority implies dominance: one individual having power over another. There can be no such dominance among equals. Dominance—force, power—must be replaced with egalitarian techniques of influence."[1]

Another family specialist lauds authority and encourages a firm no-nonsense approach when he writes: "You cannot inflict permanent damage to a child if you follow this technique: identify the rules well in advance; let there be no doubt about what is and is not acceptable behavior; when the child cold-bloodedly chooses to challenge those known boundaries in a haughty manner, give him good reason to regret it; at all times, demonstrate love and affection and kindness and understanding."[2]

What is a parent to do? To whom can he turn to gain reliable counsel? Fortunately, Scripture gives us one unfailing model. In Hebrews 12:5-13 we find God's approach to disciplining His children: *And you have forgotten the exhortation which is addressed to you as sons, My son, do not regard lightly the discipline of the Lord, nor faint when you are reproved by Him; for those whom the Lord loves He disciplines, and He scourges every son whom He receives.*

It is for discipline that you endure; God deals with you as with sons; for what son is there whom his father does not discipline?

But if you are without discipline, of which all have become partakers, then you are illegitimate children and not sons.

Furthermore, we had earthly fathers to discipline us, and we respected them; shall we not much rather be subject to the Father of spirits, and live?

For they disciplined us for a short time as seemed best to them; but He disciplines us for our good, that we may share His holiness.

All discipline for the moment seems not to be joyful, but sorrowful; yet to those who have been trained by it, afterwards it yields the peaceful fruit of righteousness.

Therefore, strengthen the hands that are weak and the knees that are feeble, and make straight paths for your feet, so that the limb which is lame may not be put out of joint, but rather be healed (Heb. 12:5-13).

Clues on How to Discipline

As we gain an understanding of how God disciplines us, we have solid clues as to how we should discipline our own children. First, note that "God looks upon discipline in a positive as well as negative light" (see vv. 7,8). He sees discipline as His obligation to guide, educate and supervise His children's choices. To be disciplined is one of the privileges of sonship. Because God cares deeply for us and because we are sons through faith in Jesus Christ, God will not fail us by neglecting our responses to life.

The parent who shirks the disciplining of his child is treating the child as if he were illegitimate (v. 8). He is saying by his neglect, "You don't belong to me. I refuse to take the responsibility for training you in decision-making. You'll just have to find out for yourself how to do it."

Second, notice that just as God is our model of how to discipline our children, our response to God's working (discipline) in our lives is a model to our sons and daughters (see Heb. 12:5). This raises some vital questions we must face:

How well disciplined am I as an adult?

How have I responded to God's corrective training program for me?

Does my life demonstrate the importance of making wise, Spirit-led decisions?

Or does my child see an undisciplined parent trying to discipline him?

For example, I teach my children to be loving toward each other. I stress the foolishness of them arguing with each other. What if they observe me in a heated discussion with their mother, or with one of them? If I am unloving, selfish and argumentative, my children will follow my example, not my words.

A Christian school teacher was counseling the mother of one of her students, but making little progress. Explaining the situation to me the teacher commented,

"She wants her daughter to be the kind of Christian she is unwilling to become herself." That mother will find it increasingly difficult to get the desired response from her daughter if she is unwilling to discipline herself.

The Father's Role in Discipline

When thinking about models for discipline, there is another key point: healthy discipline begins with the father, not the mother. A weak spot in many family situations is that most discipline is left up to the mother. This violates the biblical principle of the father being the head of the house.

I recognize that our culture makes it difficult for the father to oversee his children's discipline. Often dad must leave home early in the morning before the children are even awake. And he returns home in the evening after most of the day's activities are over. Contact with his children is limited. Obviously, the mother must handle some discipline on her own.

While I empathize with fathers in this situation the basic need remains unchanged: The father *must* provide leadership in the strategic area of discipline. What I am stressing is that the father is involved in the leadership and direction of discipline. Ephesians 6:4 directs the father to bring up the child in Christian discipline. Ideally, while the mother is the one on the scene to do much of the actual disciplining, she is following through on the discipline plan that dad has helped her work out.

One way dad can fulfill his responsibility is to build on positive discipline situations—the opportunities to guide and educate, as contrasted to the need to punish. For example, you can tell a child an open-ended story (that is, one with the ending left out) and discuss with the child the best way to cope with the situation in the story.

36

For example, you might tell your sixth-grader this story: "Bob and Jim notice that their teacher, Mr. Johnson, sometimes leaves a few coins on his desk during the day. One morning they notice a quarter on the desk. Later on, Mr. Johnson tells the class the quarter is missing and asks to have it returned. Nothing happens. Bob and Jim talk together at recess. They are both sure that the only person who was near Mr. Johnson's desk that morning was Fred. What should they do?" Then you can discuss the various possibilities with your child—should the boys talk to Mr. Johnson right away? Would that be tattling? Is tattling wrong? Should they tell Fred what they think? What if he denies he took the quarter? What if he gets mad at them?

Where Does Love Come In?

One of the crucial elements in building effective discipline is the quality of the relationship that exists between the parent and child. When we return to our master model in Scripture we find this principle stressed! "Whom the Lord loves He disciplines" (Heb. 12:6).

God does not put love in opposition to discipline; He integrates the two elements into a unity. Discipline springs from a heart of love. Discipline without love is harsh, cruel, or cold. Love without discipline is soft, sentimental, spineless. When the two are merged into a unity, discipline becomes effective for learning and growth.

To apply this principle to ourselves, as parents, we must build a strong loving bond in three directions:

1. Healthy discipline requires a strong bond of love between the parent and God. More is involved here than knowing Jesus Christ as one's personal Saviour. Parents need a quality relationship with the Lord that

allows His Spirit to guide them when difficult or sensitive issues arise. A day-by-day personal relationship with Him equips the parent to respond to the child in love rather than anger, resentment, or bitterness. Effective discipline is related to the fruit of the Spirit. As the parent walks in the Spirit he can be loving, patient, longsuffering, rather than quick-tempered and harsh (see Gal. 5:22-25).

2. Healthy discipline requires a strong bond of love between parents. With such a bond parents can work as a team in child-rearing. When parents lovingly work together their chances of being consistent in discipline are greater. They also provide better examples for their children to follow. When parents are bitter, angry, resentful or unloving with each other they are creating a poor climate for healthy discipline.

For example, Alec's parents, Joe and Marie, have had a disagreement and are not speaking to each other. Seven-year-old Alec comes into the room in a hurry and knocks over a lamp. That does it! Marie almost jerks her son out of his shoes, blisters his bottom as hard as she can and shoves him into his room. Really she is angry with her husband and her resentment has spilled over on to Alec and he catches the brunt of her feelings. Everyone suffers. Alec is confused and hurt. Joe is angry and feels that Alec was treated unfairly. Marie adds guilt to her other frustrations.

3. Healthy discipline requires a strong bond of love and understanding between parent and child. Actually, the quality of my relationship to my child is more important than the particular mode of discipline I choose to use.

If I seldom spend time with my child, show him little affection and speak to him in an impersonal manner, I lessen the chances that my discipline will be effective.

By contrast, when my child knows that I care deeply about him, he understands that if I discipline him it is because I love him. I have said to my children before a spanking, "I care about you. I have to do this because I want you to realize the seriousness of what you have done." I firmly believe that the children have understood what I was attempting to communicate.

Often a parent will discover that when he begins to neglect a child the youngster becomes more disruptive as a way of gaining attention. Recently a mother was talking to me about her young son being so disobedient and unresponsive. As we talked she came to see that she had allowed extra activities to crowd out much of the time she usually devoted to the child. When she apologized to the youngster for her neglect and began to spend more time with him again, the problems smoothed out.

When parent and child have a strong caring relationship, situations that require corrective discipline can draw the parent and child even closer together. I have observed this happen in my own home, and other parents have told me about this happening to them.

Recently our Amy was making some unwise decisions, mainly because of her lack of experience. It was necessary for me to confront Amy with the developing problem. I even had to step in and make a decision which was unpopular with her.

As we discussed what had happened and tried to understand each other, Amy shed some tears. And I'll admit that I felt twinges of typical parental doubt. Was I being fair? Was I doing this for my benefit or for Amy's own good? We struggled to a solution and while it was not pleasant, it was enriching and worthwhile. When it was settled Amy and I felt close to one another.

Hebrews 12:9 says: "We had earthly fathers to discipline us, and we respected them." What is the writer saying? It seems to me he is saying that he respected his earthly father because he knew that his father cared about him. When his father disciplined him he got the message, "He cares about me."

Healthy Discipline Grows from a Basic Plan

Is that the message that your discipline communicates to your child? I believe that there is an art to effective discipline. Constructive, positive discipline doesn't happen without plan or purpose. Every parent must guard against impulsive, rash responses that defeat his/her intended purpose. A basic plan is a guideline to keep from being carried away by your emotions.

A sound, basic plan for discipline will include the following characteristics:

1. It is constructive. Ask yourself, "Am I helping to solve the problem or am I intensifying it? Do my children find me a source of help or a source of frustration?"

2. It is carried out in love. If you are consumed with anger, get away until you can act responsibly.

3. It demonstrates a better response to a poor choice or decision. As we help them make choices, our children see us as interested in helping them with their problems, not standing in judgment of their mistakes. One of the major weaknesses with most forms of negative discipline is that it does not show the child a better way to respond; it only punishes him for what he did wrong.

4. It is consistent. When young children know what to expect they feel more secure. Ask yourself, "Do my children know what to expect from me? Am I consistent in my dealings with them?"

PARENTS' PLAN FOR ACTION

Have you thought through how you are disciplining

40

your children? Do you have a basic plan and purpose?
Are you and your spouse agreed on your plan?

Check appropriate column.   OFTEN SELDOM NEVER
1. We have a plan for disci-
   pline that is working
   well.
2. We view discipline as
   constructive and positive
   guidance, as well as corrective.
3. We spend quality time
   with our children doing
   things together each day.
4. We are consistent in
   keeping our promises to
   the children.
5. We show to our children
   genuine love and affection that carries over
   into our reason for and
   the means of discipline
   we use with our children.
6. I feel tension and disagreement over the way
   my marriage partner
   handles discipline problems.
7. Discipline is a difficult
   problem in our family.

What We Want to Do
Choose one or more from the following suggestions for
action.
1. Establish a more disciplined life-style. Our children

would observe a better example if we: (List three changes you need to make.)

2. Be more acceptant of the Lord's guidance and discipline in my life by:
   Developing a daily devotional time
   Overcoming my habit of
   Praying more honestly and frequently for guidance
   (Other desires)
3. Develop more family opportunities for fun and for doing things together.
4. Listen to my child and show him my love and acceptance.
5. Talk over with my marriage partner and decide what we want our plan for discipline to be.
6. Learn more about different views of discipline by reading *Help, I'm a Parent*,[3] by Bruce Narramore and *Dare to Discipline*[4] by James Dobson.

Footnotes

1. Rudolf Dreikurs, *Children: The Challenge* (Duell, Sloan, 1964), p. 69.
2. James Dobson, *Dare to Discipline* (Glendale: Regal Books, 1970; Wheaton: Tyndale House), p. 29.
3. Bruce Narramore, *Help, I'm a Parent* (Grand Rapids: Zondervan, 1972), pp. 55-108.
4. See footnote 2 above.

Basic Family Goal 1

To Develop Attitudes of Consistency and Self-discipline

3 Discipline— from a Plan to a Process

As you read this chapter, you will discover . . .
- how to set proper goals for discipline
- how to evaluate your motives as you discipline
- that discipline is not a series of isolated incidents but that it goes on and on, as part of the growing process

Discipline—
from a Plan to a Process

Planning for positive discipline is the beginning. The next step is getting the plan working in the everyday business of learning. How does a positive discipline design work as an ongoing process?

Setting Practical Goals

Positive discipline that works day after day must be based on practical goals that answer the needs in questions like:

Why do we bother to discipline our children?

Why not let children discover on their own and put life together for themselves?

Why not let them learn to make decisions by trial and error?

We can think of many "good" answers for these questions, but what we really need are goals. We need to know: "What am I trying to accomplish?"

When setting worthwhile goals for the discipline of our children, it helps to probe the motives behind our actions.

Negative Motives for Disciplining Children

One of the worst, but most frequent motives for disciplining is to get revenge. Your child accidentally knocks one of your expensive drinking glasses off the table, breaking it to pieces. Actually, you were partly to blame for leaving it near the edge of the table. But, you are so mad at what he did that you slap him across the face because you want revenge for the shattered glass.

Another bad motive for discipline is to prove who is boss. Sammy expresses an opinion that opposes yours. You feel threatened by his challenge to your ideas— your authority. Result? You send him to his room for being "mouthy."

A third questionable motive for discipline is to show others I'm a competent parent. After all, what will people think of us if our children don't mind? When we have friends over for dinner we want the children to say "Please," "Thank you," and "Yes, sir," because it will make us look good.

Sometimes the motive is more subtle. For example we discipline to get rid of submerged feelings. Tom and Sue have a fight over family finances. He takes the credit cards away from Sue because she has consistently overcharged the accounts. Sue resents his action. Three-year-old Laurie tugs at Sue's dress and asks several times, "Read me a book, Mommie." The underlying resentment spills over. Sue grabs Laurie, whacks her on the behind and disgustedly says, "Quit nagging me and go to your room!"

You may add other motives to this list but notice one characteristic in all of the ones I describe: They are for the parent's benefit, not the child's. When parents fail to think through their attitudes, motives and plan for discipline, they frequently "play it by ear" with disappointing results. Parents wind up satisfying their desires rather than meeting their youngster's needs.

Positive Motives for Christian Discipline

I believe that we move toward right motives when we set the right goals.

I also believe that the basic goal for Christian discipline is to always work toward enabling the child to become self-disciplined. It is necessary for your child to learn to make wise, God-honoring decisions whether you are by his side or not.

Referring back to the explanation of God's discipline in Hebrews 12:5-13, look at verse 10. God disciplines us for our good—not His. In like manner, the parent's attitude toward the disciplining of his child should be, "How can I help him know how to discipline himself?" When you can make discipline decisions from this perspective, it is good for you and your child.

What are practical ways to help your child profit from situations and move toward becoming more self-disciplined? First, it is important for the discipline process to help the child think through possible solutions and their consequences.

Suppose your child makes an unwise choice. Let's say that he disobeyed a family rule.

Punishment alone will not likely tell him why his choice was wrong. Unless the adult takes the time to help the youngster think through the fallacy of his course of action he will likely profit little.

At the core of effective discipline is an ongoing educational process. Sometimes I must teach my child something he does not know. At other times I may guide or supervise him as he attempts to make the best choice and act upon it.

The goal of discipline can more readily be achieved if we take advantage of wholesome motivators. Hebrews 12:10 describes one of God's means of motivating us to godly living. When we respond to His discipline in our lives, He allows us to share more fully in His holiness. As we demonstrate that we are trustworthy, obedient children, our loving Father allows us to experience more completely the joys of walking with Him. Many Christians continue on in a superficial Christian experience because God knows that they are too undependable, too undisciplined to handle greater opportunity and greater responsibility. However, for the person who wants to grow, to experience more of the riches in Christ Jesus, God makes this commitment: As we become obedient, self-disciplined individuals He lets us share ever more fully in the intimate life with Him.

It seems to me a Christian parent can take the same approach. As we observe our children responding positively, growing more dependable, making wise decisions we entrust greater opportunities to them. This expression of confidence challenges them to move forward to tackle other areas of responsibility. In our family experience I look for opportunities to say to the children, "You don't need to ask for permission to do that. You have proven yourself dependable."

For example, Joel has come to realize the importance

of learning how to use tools, using them carefully and then putting them away when he is finished using them. Because of this he can use most of our tools freely without asking permission each time. This is true because I wanted him to develop this independence, enough that I spent time with him teaching him basic skills. Just recently I demonstrated to him how to use a power drill properly. I've discovered by working with Joel that I help him develop both ability and responsibility.

Another example of working toward responsibility and independence is the problem we faced in deciding when to give our daughter Amy her own key to the house. Consider the three possibilities: We can give Amy a key before she really needs it, before she is able to use it responsibly. Or, we can give her a house key when she has need of it and has demonstrated trustworthiness. (Remember, we are not looking for perfection!) Or, we can make a blanket rule: "When you are 14 you can have a key."

In the first situation I placed an unfair responsibility on her. In the third situation I deny her opportunity to demonstrate her self-discipline merely because I decided to set an arbitrary date. Situation two is more motivating to the child and more profitable to the growing process. In situation two I become a supervisor, not a custodian.

In God's excellent plan He has required children to respond obediently to parents. This is wise because the young child lacks insight to understand how best to act in every situation. God, in His loving wisdom, spared children the agony of learning through costly trial and error. In effect God said, "Do what your parents tell you. I will not hold you accountable: I will hold them accountable." If my child does wrong in obedience to my instructions, I am accountable.

God's plan is not static, however. As the child matures, gaining greater understanding, the parent is to progressively release decision-making power into the growing child's hands so that he gains skill and understanding in self-discipline. The parent holds a God-given authority over the child. He has a right to expect obedience. He can, however, progressively turn over responsibility to the growing child, at which time the child by mutual agreement becomes accountable to God for that area of responsibility.

Positive Discipline—An Ongoing Process

Discipline makes more sense to me when I see it as more than a series of isolated situations which occur throughout the life of the individual. Hebrews 12:11 reminds me that discipline is a lifelong training process. Therefore, I must see individual incidents as part of a larger picture.

When two of my children begin picking at each other, I can glibly say, "All kids are like that," or I can recognize an area of their lives that needs help. I can mentally plan a long-term approach to helping them build respect for each other, as well as teach them how to resolve personal differences from a Christian perspective.

Recognizing that discipline is an ongoing process helps me in another way. I become more patient with individual situations because I realize that these are the teaching opportunities I need to help my child form attitudes toward life. As we discuss why a certain decision was wise or unwise the child gains insight into what makes a decision good or bad. When we talk about why a situation went wrong I want my child to understand what should have been done so he will know the right response when he faces that situation again.

Some effective parents practice discipline like a wise

49

teacher grades a test. The child may have failed the test; however, the teacher sits down with the child, goes over the test material, discusses the errors made, and helps the student understand how to avoid making the same error again. I recall a number of incidents—even in graduate school—when a teacher would give a test and never return the test. I had no opportunity to discover what I had not learned properly, which left me frustrated. I am sure that in the same way parents often leave their child frustrated by not explaining to him what he did wrong or why what he did was in error. The wise parent will take time to discuss with the child where he has erred and show him how to make a better response so that he can succeed the next time.

In Hebrews 12:11 we are reminded of another aspect of the training process: "All discipline for the moment seems not to be joyful, but sorrowful; yet to those who have been trained by it, afterwards it yields the peaceful fruit of righteousness." It seems to me that this early Christian teaching reminds us that many discipline situations are unpleasant both for the one being disciplined and the one doing the disciplining. The wise parent must realize, however, that confronting the situation and dealing with it lovingly, wisely and thoroughly will bear fruit in the future. This fruit can be most encouraging.

We can paraphrase Hebrews 12:11 in these words: "Right now it is not pleasant to deal with this problem. Yet, I know that if my child can gain insight and be more adequately trained through it, this situation will bear fruit in the days ahead." Viewing discipline as a life process is essential.

1. Be aware of your own limitations. Learn to recognize that when your patience is wearing thin it will be more difficult for you to handle discipline situations

constructively. When you are weary discipline is more difficult to handle. Also, recognize tendencies toward favoritism. A quiet, gentle child may be given privileges denied the robust, energetic, talkative child because you subtly judge quietness as a desirable virtue. (This is not necessarily true.) Likewise, be aware of tendencies toward being too severe or too lax in punishment.

2. Recognize that your approach to discipline should vary according to children's needs. Consistency is not to be equated with rigidity. Some children are more sensitive than others. In the same manner you should not be treating a fourteen-year-old like a four-year-old.

3. Avoid corrective measures which are humiliating, degrading, or shameful. Parents are to respect the feelings and ego of the child. Corrective discipline is a private affair between parent and child.

4. Recognize the danger of disciplining in anger. The typical Christian parent must admit that there have been times when he disciplined his children in anger. However, if this is always the pattern there are problems involved. First, your child sees you venting your wrath on him. When you lose control you demonstrate your lack of discipline. Many Scripture passages in the book of Proverbs counsel against the person who cannot cope properly with anger (see Prov. 14:29; 15:1,18; 16:32; 10:11). Second, your child does not see punishment for wrong but your loss of temper. The focus is wrong. Third, the power of effective discipline is when the child sees that you love him. "The last thing I want to do is spank you. But, because I love you I must." Some readers will have difficulty believing that this can occur but I assure you that it can.

So what's the solution? Well, I'm going to share with you what I try to practice—though sometimes I fail. But, when I do practice it, it does not fail. When a situation occurs which prompts anger in me, I try to say, "Go to your room; I'm angry and need time to think and pray." I get alone and pray out the anger. Then I can go to the child and deal with him without wrong motives. I can verify that this is a workable solution if you have consistently maintained a healthy parent-child relationship. If, however, the relationship has deteriorated to the point where distrust and resentment exist, it may take time for the child to realize that your motives are sincere.

PARENT'S PLAN FOR ACTION

Now, is your opportunity to transfer the plan into the process as you, as parents, try to determine the discipline patterns that exist in your own family and work together toward positive Christian discipline.

Where We Are Now

Check appropriate column.   ALWAYS OFTEN SELDOM NEVER

1. I discipline my children because what they do makes me mad.
2. I discipline my children to show them who is boss in the home.
3. I discipline my children so that other people won't think that I'm a poor parent.
4. I discipline my children because of underlying feelings I cannot handle.
5. I discipline my children because I want them to become self-disciplined.

Identify and evaluate typical discipline situations in your home, as well as the way you respond. Even more profitable may be your plan to choose a more effective form of discipline. Complete the exercise below with this in mind.

TYPICAL SITUATIONS	MY TYPICAL RESPONSE	A BETTER WAY
Example: child habitually spills milk at table	Get mad at child. Tell him not to be so clumsy.	Accept child's lack of coordination as normal, help child learn where to place glass, teach him to use two hands, etc.

What We Want to Do

List the goals that you want to achieve in the child's life as indications of his becoming self-disciplined. The examples are representative. Add others which you desire to work toward.

CHILD AT 5	CHILD AT 10	CHILD AT 15
Responsible to dress self; personal hygiene	Able to care for room; share decisions in choice of clothing	Able to purchase clothes wisely; able to choose friends wisely; developing Bible study skills

Basic Family Goal 2

To Develop an Atmosphere of Love and Unity

4 How to Build Good Relationships with Your Child

As you read this chapter, you will discover . . .

- the most vital part of parenting—building good relationships
- why your children can read you like a book
- why admitting your own faults to your children won't destroy their respect for you
- how to improve the quality of time spent with family members
- how to reevaluate your concerns in light of your child's concerns

How to Build Good Relationships with Your Child

Most young couples who are "expecting" prepare carefully for the glad event. Outwardly, everything appears ready. Baby's room is newly painted. The crib is spotless. Diapers are already neatly folded and stored. The doctor has carefully briefed the expectant mother on what to anticipate during delivery. In many situations, dad has been coached on delivery procedures and what he can do to assist (and/or) support his wife.

Yet most parents-to-be are not really ready for the birth of their child. Why? Because they have little or no training in child-rearing. Most likely they have never identified forces in their lives that will hinder or help them in their task. Parents usually have hazy aspirations for their children but no clear plan for how to accomplish these goals. They want to be "good" parents but often do not have clear ideas on what a "good" parent is or does, or what personal changes are necessary to become that person.

Stop and think about it. How well prepared were you for the arrival of a child in your home? What goals or aspirations did you have? What skills had you mastered? As you look back, what help do you wish that you had received? What do you feel are the really important aspects of parenthood?

The Parental Bond

From experience with parenting our five children, I am convinced the most vital part of parenthood is the quality of the relationship that exists between the parent and the child. A satisfying quality relationship does not just happen. The parent must do certain things to build and nurture a strong, comfortable bond. For example, during the first year of his life a child receives his most crucial perceptions about the world he has entered. He usually gains these perceptions through his mother. When he is gently and lovingly handled he senses the kindness of other persons. When he feels the warmth of the mother's body in a relaxed, tension-free situation, he perceives that a secure, satisfying evironment surrounds him. He begins to trust the people in his life, especially his mother.

Fathers can also build a loving relationship with a newborn child. Unfortunately, most men never realize how much they can contribute to their infant's development. When a dad gently holds his youngster and talks to him, the child becomes aware of his father's love and more gradually becomes aware of two people who surround him with warm, positive feelings. It is during these early months of a child's life that both parents lay the foundation for their lifelong relationship with their child.

It is awesome to realize how strategic the early expressions of affection and attention are to the infant's growth. Numerous studies stress the fact that the child who is denied warmth and love in early life suffers serious consequences. These studies generally agree that the child's physical, intellectual and social development is almost always retarded when deprived of maternal care, and that symptoms of physical and mental illness may appear.

In the light of such sobering research, every parent should think twice about the cost of being too busy to take time to play with, love and cuddle his little one. It is my belief that even the most inexperienced parent can become skillful in creating a rich, productive relationship with his children. It takes time—lots of time—but it pays huge dividends. Your relationship to your child is the key to his character formation, to his response to discipline, to his very personality. This is a key question every parent must answer: How can I build a relationship with my child which will enrich his life and mine?

Steps to Enrich the Parental Bond

The following five steps are ones you can take to build a healthy relationship with your son and/or daughter. With each step are suggestions for practical ways to make these steps part of your family life.

1. Become Aware of Your Underlying Attitudes

Adults do not always realize how they feel about children and how their feelings affect their attitudes and actions. For example:

IF I FEEL THIS WAY	I MAY ACT THIS WAY
Children are to be seen and not heard.	I ignore my 7-year-old while talking to a friend at the super-market.
Kids don't really know much.	I am impatient when he can't seem to learn his multiplication tables.
A child is a nuisance to be endured.	I call him clumsy for spilling his milk.
I've more important things to do than play with my kid.	I make excuses about having work to do when he wants us to play to-gether with the building blocks.
I work hard all day and deserve some peace and quiet.	I hide behind a news-paper and grunt "Uh huh" without hearing what he says.
A child cannot think for himself.	I tell him that he is too little to choose what clothes he wants to wear.
My friends will judge me	I pinch my 2-year-old

for the way my children act.	because he won't sit still in church, though I know at two he can't sit still.
Men should never show emotions—that's a sign of weakness.	I never kiss or hug my little boy.
Only sissies cry.	I say, "Quit your crying or I'll give you something to really cry about!"

The above lists are only possibilities, but they illustrate something vital in parenting. Underlying attitudes really do influence our actions. Frequently, we are not even aware of our attitudes. But our children are. Children are exceptionally skillful in sensing disguised attitudes and motives in adults. Young children pick up our cues and interpret them in very personal ways.

In short, children see right through their parents. Instinctively they know if daddy goes along with their make-believe or the game they want to play. Unerringly, they feel mom's wholeheartedness (or lack of same) as she reads the story aloud. And as they read us like the open books that we are, our children think, "Daddy likes me. He likes to have fun with me," or "I'm a nuisance to Mommy. She doesn't like me."

The point is, you may not be aware of the messages you are sending your child. He may be receiving what you have no intention of sending. Your underlying attitudes—not necessarily spoken—can drive your child away from you rather than draw him to you.

I recall visiting in a home where a Christian father

didn't know how to relate to his son. He never showed him any affection. Although he talked freely with adults he seldom spoke with his son. When he did speak to his son it was usually to criticize for something he had done. The result? A relationship that deteriorated as the boy grew older. Eventually the boy rebelled and brought much heartache to the whole family.

As I talked with one Christian father, he confessed, "I have no patience with my two boys. Time after time, sooner or later, I blow my top . . . " I encouraged this father first by admitting that I had had a similar problem, especially when tired or under pressure. And then we went on to talk about the strength in admitting a lack of patience. By recognizing our weakness, we could more realistically seek God's power to change us.

Too frequently the parent fails to recognize the needy areas of his own life and passes the blame on to his child. We may be naggers or we easily lose our temper. Perhaps we are disorganized. The important point is to face up to our own deficiency, seek God's grace and not blame our children for our faults!

And don't be afraid to be honest. You won't lose your child's respect if you say, "I'm sorry I blew my top this morning. I was wrong about what happened. It was my fault for letting my temper get out of hand."

Key phrases that build solid relationships of 14-karat love: "I'm sorry . . . " "I was wrong . . . " "It was my fault."

Try them. Your kids will like them, and in the long run, so will you. Like the time I was "confessing" a weakness to Amy and she replied, "That's okay, Dad. We all have trouble in that area."

These words spoken by Jesus should be burned into the heart of each and every parent: "(The) mouth speaks from that which fills the heart" (Luke 6:45).

What do our children hear coming from our hearts by way of our mouths? Do our words convey disinterest, bitterness, resentfulness, suspicion?

"Well, if you feel we must, we must . . . "

"Can't you see I'm busy? . . . later maybe . . . "

"What have you been into this time?"

Or do our words carry affirmation, thoughtfulness, warmth?

"I'm really pleased with that report card!"

"Would you like me to go with you or do you want to handle it alone?"

"You're really somebody special to me!"

"I appreciate your thoughtfulness."

Scripture tells us that "The (human) heart is more deceitful than all else and is desperately sick . . . " (Jer. 17:9). But Scripture also promises the Christian parent the help and power of the Holy Spirit which produces " . . . love, joy, peace, patience, kindness, goodness, faithfulness, gentleness, self-control"—all the things a parent needs! (See Gal. 5:22,23.)

To build quality relationships with your children, build a quality relationship with Christ. Seek the reality of His presence. Walk in the Spirit and your mouth will be an instrument of blessing, not a weapon. To paraphrase Luke 6:45: "What fills my mouth comes from my heart."

2. Establish Correct Priorities

If you want to build life-enriching relationships with your children give them top priority in your schedule of responsibilities and activities. Yes, top priority. Parents feel the pressure of many commitments. Dad wants to act responsibly on the job. He would like to get ahead. Often, he works extra hours, comes home tired, uptight, preoccupied. Billy pops in and says, "Play ball, Dad!"

62

Dad groans and plays dead instead. Billy goes off alone to develop a warm relationship with his bat.

Mom is actively involved in a women's Bible study. She sings in the choir, and teaches a Sunday School class. She works part-time as a salesperson. Tricia comes to her after supper saying, "Mommie, read to me." Mom says, over her shoulder on the way out, "Gotta get to choir practice." And Tricia is left again to build a growing relationship with the 23-inch surrogate mother in the family room.

One study of 200 seventh- and eighth-grade boys revealed that the average time spent between father and son was seven and a half minutes per week. Building lasting relationships takes a little longer than that!

I once asked a missionary what he would do differently if he could live his life over. After a brief pause he said, "I'd spend more time with my children. I really regret not having done that."

Stop right now and analyze how you are using your time. Complete the time indicator chart at the end of this chapter. Then answer the following question:

"Can I identify a specific time each day when I am able to relate to each of my children in a personal, meaningful manner, such as, going for a walk together, reading a book, swinging on the swing?"

I find it helpful to think in terms of specific time spots reserved for each child. The half hour before or after the evening meal can be used to good advantage. Bedtime is another excellent time to share with the child. When Jody was young, my wife, Winnie, would read to her after the older children were in bed for the night. Jody knew that she could count upon having that time with her mother.

For example, the other night I stretched out on the bed with Joel and asked him how things were going at school. He related a frustration he was experiencing and in the conversation that followed he discovered a solution. He also went to sleep more peacefully.

Another practical way to assure time for family members is to develop a family calendar. Pencil in those time commitments to each family member. Once a commitment to a family member has been made, attempt to honor it at all costs. When someone asks you for time which conflicts with your family commitment merely tell him, "I have an important previous engagement." Even as I write this I realize the weight of what I am saying. Amy and I have a date to go bike riding Friday after lunch. I also have a commitment to help Joel repair his bike tire tonight after dinner.

Discovering and using priority time with family members is a key to effective parenting. Building relationships takes time. You as a parent must program time with family members into your busy schedule. Our children belong high on our list of priorities. They represent one of the few enduring investments that we can make in life.

3. Choose Quality over Quantity

All right, suppose you reserve time for family members, what will you do together? Will you make quality use of that time? For example, you and your child might spend two hours together watching TV, yet this would likely be poor quality use of time. Quality use of time involves one basic question: Can I devote my complete attention to my child? (Or is my mind on other matters?)

Time with our children will involve a variety of situations with many levels of intensity. Jody regularly goes to the grocery store with me. Winnie and Amy often cook together in the kitchen. After supper, Joel and I play ball in the cul-de-sac. At bedtime Amy questions me about the Trinity. Our whole family sings together as we travel in the automobile. In each situation I must be alert to opportunities to share in a significant manner with each child. For one it may be a bit of information. Another may want assurance that he can accomplish some task. Another may merely desire adult friendship and understanding. The more sensitive I am to their needs the higher the quality of our relationship.

Find regular time slots in your daily schedule which are consistently reserved for specific family members. This will not rule out spontaneous events but rather provide the foundation upon which your parent-child relationship is being built. The years of early childhood are especially important in building relationships, for as children enter the teen years the family finds it more difficult to be together. Young people are busy with their activities and parents are frequently involved with outside commitments. Thus, the early years of family life can be especially valuable years in deepening relationships.

I have found that one good way to find specific times for my children is to know what interests them. I had to develop skill in establishing routines or patterns, but also to discover common interests in which we could play, share and work together. For this reason I constructed a "Family Interest Indicator" (see end of this chapter) to help me discover points of common interest that our family members share.

The "Family Interest Indicator" will help you evaluate your family's basis of mutual sharing. For example, mother and son may both share an interest in stamp collecting. As they work together on the stamp album, they learn, share and enjoy—all the while building a solid parent-child relationship. Right now Joel is showing interest in playing a baritone ukulele. Since I know how to play one we can share meaningful time together as I teach him to play.

Opportunities to work on long-term projects, hobbies, or interests do not always exist. Seek to discover activities that are valuable short-term events. For example, this morning Winnie asked the older children to help her put a puzzle together. I took a break and joined with them as they worked on the task.

4. Reevaluate Your "Concerns"

As you seek stronger parent-child relationships you may need to reevaluate your concern. By this I mean the way you see things and the way your child sees them. I think that they represent the issues around which you are building the relationship. It seems to me the relationship is built around the child's performance or his person. The parent's performance concerns frequently are expressed to the child by commands:

"Pick up the junk in your room!"

"I've told you twenty times to wipe off your feet when you come in the house!"

"Sit up straight!"

Mentally switch roles with your child for a moment. It should help you realize how unsatisfying it is to be the "buck private"—always commanded by someone else.

I believe that "concerns" are crucial ground for all parents. Some parents sound like drill sergeants trying to shape up the troops. Colossians 3:21 reminds us that a father can frustrate his child and make him lose heart. If you have been playing "drill sergeant" or "commander" resign your commission right now. That doesn't mean you abdicate authority or cop out on your responsibility. It does mean that you try to emphasize the positive out of concern based on love.

66

One of your chief concerns should be your child's concerns.

"Do my parents like me as much as they do my brother?" (He wants to know that someone cares about him.)

"Will Mom come back?" (He is concerned that home is a place of security.)

"What can we do that will be fun?" (He is concerned about having a good time.)

When I take time to help Annette put a puzzle together, I am letting her know that I realize that she likes to have fun. I make Annette's concern my concern.

What about your child? Does he/she like puzzles? Or perhaps it's playing the piano, taking walks, shooting baskets, riding his bike, reading books. Look for your child's concerns. They are points of contact you must use to build a good relationship.

This may not be easy at first, but you can develop the skill as you go along. Keep a mental inventory. Better yet jot things down. Take time to learn about your child's interests. When you purchase gifts for him let them reflect your awareness of what he likes. For example, can you name your youngster's favorite color, favorite food, favorite friend, favorite place, etc.? Focus your attention on your child's personal life.

Why not try making two lists, one entitled "My Concerns for My Child" and the other "My Child's Concerns." Compare the lists. How could you discover more of his interests and concerns?

5. Become Sensitive to Nonverbal Communication

Nonverbal communication is the "body language" that usually speaks more forcefully than any words we use. It is our tone of voice, the look in our eyes, the posture of our body. For example, Joey is disappointed at not being included in the neighborhood gang. His dad

67

didn't notice his downcast look, his drooping shoulders.

Or, Michelle is fearful when her mother says that she is going to be away for a few days. But mother doesn't notice when Michelle comes to her with an anxious look in her eyes. In both of these situations the parents do not detect the nonverbal signals their children are sending. If they did they could help their children constructively cope with what is bothering them.

I believe that this basic sensitivity to the life of the child is a very important dimension to effective parenting. Many well-meaning adults fail to sense disappointment, frustration, loneliness, and a host of other feelings in the child. They cannot read the signals that their youngsters send.

Here are some signals my children send out to me:

Annette crawls up on my lap to say: "I want attention."

Jody will take my hand in the store to make herself feel more secure. (Interestingly enough Annette, who is younger, lets loose because she wants to be independent and explore.)

Joel sighs forcefully when he is provoked or disgusted.

Amy begins to cry when she feels deeply about something.

Children are real persons. They appreciate someone who understands; someone who listens; someone who helps them sort out their feelings. If you develop this ability to understand and empathize with your child's feelings you will inevitably strengthen the relationship between the two of you.

PARENTS' PLAN FOR ACTION

To profit from this chapter you should plan to work with the evaluation/planning pages that follow. You may be tempted to put this off until later. But if you will complete these pages promptly you and your child will be the ones who gain and enjoy the results.

Where We Are Now

Discover where your family is on sharing time and interests by completing the "Time and Interest Indicator" chart at the end of this chapter. What interests do members of your family share? Do you consciously make plans to spend time together?

What We Want to Do

At the end of this chapter is a "Family Time Plan Sheet." Use this to plan the coming week or two with family members. Check off the activity you plan for a day that seems appropriate (from what you know now about the family's schedule.) If several family members are involved, initial which ones will take part in the different activities. If none of the activities mentioned fit in with your family's needs pencil in things that seem right for your family. The activities need not be elaborate. They should meet the following criteria:

1. The activity allows us to spend quality time with each other.
2. It is interesting to us—at least to try one time.
3. The activity is appropriate for the ages of the people in our family.
4. The activity is suitable for the amount of time we have to spend.

Praying for God's guidance in building happy family relationships doesn't have to wait! Talk over when you and your spouse can spend some time today talking with God about the people in your home and the time you spend together. As you pray, praise Him for each person in your family.

69

FAMILY TIME INDICATOR

Instructions: Place the initial of family members who spend time together in the specific activity identified, as well as the amount of time spent.

Weekdays	Weekends	Activity
		Breakfast together
		Lunch together
		Supper together
		Read aloud
		Recreation
		● Camping
		● Home recreation
		● Away recreation
		Regular travel time together
		● To church, shopping, etc.
		Hobbies
		Designated family night
		Working around house or yard
		Other _____

Evaluation: Does the indicator suggest (1) you do not have ample time together? (2) certain family members are neglected (unequal distribution of time)?

FAMILY TIME PLAN SHEET

Instructions: Check appropriate boxes for time-activity you plan to share in together.

S	M	T	W	T	F	S	Activity
							Eat meal together
							Read book
							Go camping, fishing
							Work on mutual hobby, interest
							Begin a family ministry
							Go window shopping
							Start a family project
							Play games, recreation
							Watch and **discuss** choice TV programs
							Prepare special snack, meal
							Picnic at park, beach, etc.
							Plan special time of family worship
							Sing together
							Hike, bike or **walk** together
							Play miniature golf
							Eat out (MacDonalds, etc.)
							Honor day for family member
							Tell story of your childhood

FAMILY INTEREST INDICATOR

Instructions: Beside each item write the names of family members who share that identical interest.

Family Members' Names	Ways We Plan to Share Interests	Activity
		Talents
		Hobbies
		Sports
		Christian ministry
		Recreation
		Reading
		● History
		● Bible study
		● Etc.
		Cooking
		Yard/Gardening
		Care of pets
		Other _____
		_____
		_____
		_____
		_____

Basic Family Goal 2

To Develop an Atmosphere of Love and Unity

5 How to Communicate with Your Child

As you read this chapter, you will discover . . .
- why good parent-child communication doesn't "just happen"
- reasons parents and children misunderstand each other
- when to start building healthy communication
- the part attitude plays in building strong communication lines
- how to plan for improving parent-child communication skills

How to Communicate with Your Child

Billy comes bounding into the house with a troubled look on his face.

"Mom, where did I come from?" he asks.

For a minute Billy's mother panics wondering just how to begin telling him the facts of life, then with a determined look she says, "Now Billy . . ."

After listening to Mom for a minute, Billy indignantly exclaims, "No, no, not that! Mark said he came from Ohio and I want to know where I came from!"

It isn't always easy to sense what a child really means

or to understand what is behind the questions he asks. But, if you are going to build good parent-child communication, it is important to take time and try to discover what he is thinking, what he is asking and to talk about what is on your youngster's mind.

Reasons We Misunderstand Each Other

Clear, effective communication between you and your child won't "just happen." Too many barriers and gaps exist between parent and child for communication to be automatic—without any effort.

First there is the vocabulary gap. Often a child does not understand the words his parents use. One chilly day when our Jody was about three I told her to get her maroon jacket and we would go for a walk. Jody just stood there looking at me with a puzzled expression. Finally I realized I had confused Jody with the word maroon. She didn't know what I was talking about. Sure, I was talking to Jody, but I wasn't communicating.

There is also an age gap. Parents not only forget that their child has a limited vocabulary compared to theirs, they also forget what it is like to view the world through a child's eyes.

Do you remember how excited you could be over a candy bar or a new pair of shoes when you were a child? Do you remember how new words and unfamiliar ideas confused you or how puzzling it was when adults gave you instructions you couldn't understand? These are the kind of feelings that create the age gap.

Not long ago when I was trying to talk something over with our daughter Amy she expressed some of the frustration caused by the age gap when she said, "Oh, Dad, you don't understand. You're just a parent."

Actually, the age gap exists because of the parallel experience gap. Parents view life and talk about things from a rich background of experiences that the child does not have. The other day I discovered how real the experience gap is when Joel and his 11-year-old friend wanted to go fishing alone. I could see the dangers involved because of my experiences on numerous fishing trips. But because of his limited experience, Joel had real difficulty understanding or accepting the fact that the planned adventure could be potentially dangerous. Only as I stopped to think about the situation from Joel's perspective could I communicate effectively with him.

Another reason parents and children sometimes fail to understand each other is that they "tune out" the other person. Parents who are constantly exposed to the chatter and noise of their children frequently "tune out" what is going on around them. The child, too, grows so accustomed to his parents telling him what to do and what not to do that he anticipates what his mom or dad will say and does not listen carefully. The result? No real communication.

Often I have asked one of my children to get me something in another part of the house—off the workbench, for example—only to have the child come back and say, "I can't find it." When I take time to talk things over with the youngster I frequently discover that he/she didn't really listen or hear me in the first place.

Communication Begins at Birth

Long before your infant is able to speak words he can sense your feelings for him. He enjoys your response to his sounds and expressions. And it doesn't take long for him to learn to value your warm, cheerful voice. The parent who reaches out to the child with many verbal and nonverbal expressions of tenderness and love is laying a good foundation for healthy parent-child communication.

If your child is yet an infant, practice talking to him even though he cannot understand what you are saying. Watch his response. The sound of your voice and the sight of your smile conveys your love and your desire to relate to him. All of this is important to his development. When you respond to his "cooing" and "squealing" you tell him that he is worthwhile and that you care about what he "says."

Attitudes Speak Louder than Words

No matter how old your child is, your attitude is a vital factor in establishing good communication. As Luke 6:45 says: "(The) mouth speaks from that which fills the heart."

I can remember when our Jody was about three and had the rich imagination of early childhood. She would frequently tell us about her adventures with a favorite teddy bear, Smokey. We listened to her conversations about Smokey carefully, even asking her questions. We saw these times as opportunities for us to slip into Jody's world with her for a few minutes. Never treat lightly your child's world of imagination. Your interested, participating attitude invites your child to share his/her interests and happiness along with fears and problems.

Maintaining an attitude that encourages communication means that the parent respects that child's feelings and doesn't "put the child down." For example, youngsters who become discouraged value a person who will listen understandingly—without giving a sermon. Children sometimes feel misunderstood by their peers but if they feel sure their parents respect and care for them they will often seek out mom or dad for understanding. Be sensitive to your child when he comes to you to share something that's happened to him. He needs your attitude of respect and caring.

An important factor in communicating well with your child is being able to accept the disagreements as a part of everyday life. You say it is bedtime. Your child says he is not sleepy. Although you feel you must insist on your child going to bed, this is an opportunity for you to acknowledge your child's feelings. Maybe you will allow him to look at a few of his/her favorite books, listen to a quiet record, or spend a little time talking with you.

Parent-child communication is greatly strengthened when your attitude and the home atmosphere is friendly. Your child needs to feel comfortable with you, assured he is enjoyed and cared about, not merely endured. But it is not always easy for adults to maintain a friendly, warm attitude in the home. Why? Most parents are involved in a very busy schedule and it is all too easy to convey to a family member, "Go away and don't bother me. I'm too busy. I've more important things to do right now."

How easy it is to communicate an attitude of disinterest and unfriendliness to a child! From my experience I believe there are four key reasons for this:

Parents get too busy.

Parents feel that children have nothing really valuable or sensible to say.

Parents believe that children do not have real or significant problems.

Often, parents forget the reality of their own childhood.

When you are aware of these common pitfalls you can plan for ways to create a friendly, warm feeling. The simple everyday ways are best. A smile or a loving arm around your child's shoulder can be an invitation to, "Tell me about it." Learn to initiate conversations with questions or comments that show your interest, like:

"Tell me about your field trip today."

"How did you feel when that man yelled at you?"

"Describe your new teacher to me."

"Show me how it works."

These are the kind of requests that are friendly knocks at the door of a child's heart.

Discovering Meanings

The world of the young child is filled with things that are new and strange. Day by day the youngster is confronted with new routines, new words, new people and new discoveries. But often, parents do not sense the "newness" of their youngster's experiences because they themselves are familiar with what is happening.

The following suggestions are to make you aware of some of the needs your child has as he tries to find meaning for his new experiences.

Earlier in this chapter we talked about the child's limited vocabulary making communication difficult at times. When you use words that are new to your child, do you make sure he understands? For example, when you give him directions it is a good idea to ask your child to tell you what he heard you say. This will be easier for him if you remember to use short sentences. Long, complex sentences are confusing to a youngster.

Children have a limited understanding of the words they use. You have had years to build up associations and shades of meaning . . . your child is just in the process of doing this. To make certain you and your child understand each other it is a good idea to compare mental images. One of the most effective ways to do this is to ask the child to draw you a picture of what you have been talking about. Then you take a turn and draw a picture showing your idea of something the child said. You can have fun drawing pictures together and talking about meanings. Such an experience can help both you and your child communicate with greater accuracy and understanding.

Many times children use words without knowing what they mean. Frequently, I ask one of my children to explain a word I hear one of them use. It's not uncommon for me to get an answer like "I don't know." Or sometimes, to get an inaccurate definition. You can help your children develop a better understanding by talking about words they use but do not seem to fully understand. For example, think through how you would help a child who gave you one of the following definitions:

Salvation: a whole bunch of people, like an army (10-year-old); going to church (8-year-old); truck that collects useful things (10-year-old).

Virgin: a lady of olden times (10-year-old).

Witness: swim in pool and get all wet (7-year-old).

Christian parents frequently talk to their children in symbolic terms: a black heart; let your light shine; soul; fishers of men; etc. Remember that young children think very literally; so when you share a biblical truth, use words and concepts that are clear to your child.[1]

PARENTS' PLAN FOR ACTION

To start building healthy communication within your own family structure, begin to plan for improvement by strengthening your own positive attitudes and by creating a friendly home atmosphere.

Where We Are Now

Evaluate the effectiveness of your communication with your child by completing the following test. Place your child's name in the blank space as you read each statement. Check the appropriate response.

1. I sit down with＿＿＿＿＿＿and encourage him/her to talk with me.
2. I am sensitive when＿＿＿＿＿is discouraged, restless, troubled or silent.
3. I interrupt＿＿＿＿＿when he/she is talking.
4. I am sarcastic to＿＿＿＿＿.
5. I enjoy listening to＿＿＿＿＿talk.
6. I tend to speak to＿＿＿＿＿in commands: "Be quiet," "Eat your food," etc.
7. When dealing with problems in ＿＿＿＿＿'s life I use words which attack the child rather than the problem.

What We Want to Do
Choose two of the following activities to work on.
1. Circle the item in the test which you would like to work on. List two specific actions you can take to improve in this area.
2. List 15 different ways to say "I love you" to your child.
   Here are three examples to get you started:
   a. Fix his favorite food.
   b. Make a poster to creatively say it.
   c. Invite him to go to the store with you to get an ice-cream cone.
3. Make two lists: "When I am a good listener" and "When I am a poor listener." Choose an item from each list that you want to work with this week.
4. Get a group of 2-4 persons. Ask them to jot down two adjectives to describe the following objects as they visualize them in their mind: automobile, chair, love, dad, house. How widely do their mental images differ? What does this tell you about communication?
5. Plan to spend at least 15 minutes each day listening to your child talk. Try to identify with his point of

81

view. What does he talk about? How long are his sentences? What words does he use?

Footnote

1. A uniquely clear and helpful example for guiding a child toward Jesus has been prepared by Wesley Haystead in his book for Christian parents and teachers titled *You Can't Begin Too Soon* (Regal, 1974). How to communicate what it means to become a child of God—a member of God's family—is illustrated in chapter 6 of his book, particularly in the section titled "Guiding the young child toward Jesus," pages 104-107.

The colorful, appealing booklet titled *God Wants You to Be a Member of His Family* (Gospel Light Publications, 1972) is another helpful resource for communicating with a child the biblical truths able to make him "wise unto salvation" (2 Tim. 3:15).

The Magic Merry-Go-Round is a delightful little storybook by Gilbert Beers (Moody, 1973) into which is woven the vital truth of boys and girls entering into a personal relationship with Jesus Christ, the Saviour.

Basic Family Goal 3

To Provide Opportunities to Grow, Discover, Create

6 How to Help Your Child Learn

As you read this chapter, you will discover ...
- how your child learns
  —from you
  —from his or her environment
  —from firsthand experiences
  —from vicarious experiences
  —from asking questions
  —from play experiences
- that your child learns at his own speed and in his own way

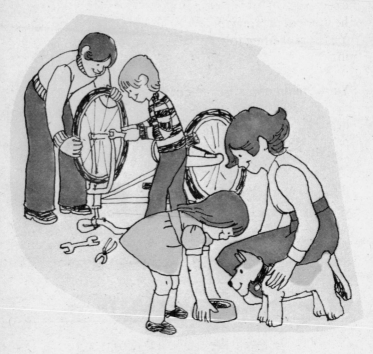

How to Help Your Child Learn

Exploring, manipulating, inquiring, creating. Putting together, taking apart. Stacking up, knocking down. Tasting, smelling, feeling, looking, listening. What potential rests in your child. Potential to be released, guided, and encouraged. How thrilling to be able to share with God in the training of a child!

If we are to cooperate with the Spirit of God in the development of our young child it is important to grasp the principles of how a child learns. Children learn the way God designed them to learn—from their everyday experiences. And it is important for parents to know how to cooperate with and to participate in the process. Yes, it is exciting to realize that your youngster is learning.

Your Child Learns from You

A significant amount of the child's learning occurs at home in informal conversations and situations when the parent may not be aware that he is "teaching" and the child is learning.

Children can learn to enjoy words and ways to use them imaginatively. If our children develop a rich vocabulary it will likely be because Winnie and I try to use a rich and varied vocabulary in our everyday conversations with them. In their conversations they then try out new words they have heard us use.

Children learn as you share ideas with them. Educators have discovered that parents greatly influence the child's cognitive development in the early years of life. Parents are laying the foundation for the children's school years when they share ideas, experiences and events with their child beginning in his preschool years. The child's learning experiences in the classroom are later enriched or limited when the youngster starts school to the degree his mind has been fertilized and stimulated as a young child.

Parents can maximize the benefit of everyday learning experiences with their child. For example, taking time to show your child the different shapes of vegetables or fruits is the foundation for his learning to observe similarities and differences. Even identifying their color by name helps him grasp a fundamental concept. Recently I "tore down" an automobile engine to repair it. In the process Joel became intrigued about various engine parts. We discussed what various parts are called and the functions they perform. Through this process Joel developed awareness of the basic parts of an automobile engine.

Last night we decided to view some of our family slides. As I began to set up the projector, Joel asked, "Dad, can I operate the projector?" Then Amy and Jill asked if they could, too. My first inner reaction was that I should do it. It would be easier, less risky, less complicated. However, a second, wiser response occurred when I realized that it would be more profitable for them if with my instruction they could operate the machine. The second thought won out!

Our children learn from us. They learn from the whole range of the words we use, how we use them, the attitudes we express, the situations we explore, and the information we share. We do well to evaluate what we are teaching.

Your Child Learns from His Environment

How boring it must be to be an animal in a zoo. So restricted in movement. Every day the same old thing. No challenge; no change of scenery; no place to go.

Some homes are like that. A barren land with little to stimulate the mind or arouse curiosity. It need not be that way. Home can be a rich environment with many objects and experiences to learn from. Things to touch, feel, smell, taste, and listen to.

Children of most any age can develop a keen appetite for books, but this seldom occurs unless someone opens doors of exploration. Then books can become doorways to adventure, exploration, imagination and discovery. In like manner children enjoy building with scraps of wood, fruit and vegetable cans, or cardboard boxes, but someone must provide such resources to satisfy the youngsters' curiosity.

Do you realize how intensely the young child hungers to learn? Watch him as he explores the house from corner to corner. He delights in unwinding the toilet paper, pulling out the pots and pans, eating the dog food, feeling the texture of the screen door, or chewing the corner of a misplaced book. He's not trying to frustrate you, although he probably does. It's his irresistible urge to understand more about his world.

One lesson we have learned is that children need a home planned for their needs. If you want your child to grow intellectually you need to put resources within reach to stimulate his cognitive development. Thus, you must decide whether you will have the neatest house on the block, or the one most enjoyable in which to live and learn.

Parents can help the child understand and appreciate his environment. Dad may help Billy become more discerning by asking him to discover items in a magazine picture. Mom may help him explore the concept of alikeness and difference through items of varying color, texture, size and shape in the kitchen. Flowers in the yard may be a medium for discovering the wonders of color. Dogs, cats, birds, fish, etc., are excellent for teaching attitudes toward God's creatures, as well as the marvel of creation. Teaching situations are available all around you. Take advantage of them while your children are in their early years.

Your Child Learns from Firsthand Experiences

Healthy children are doers. They profit most when they are given opportunities to personally experience ideas. For instance, it is more meaningful for the child to plant a seed and see it grow into a lovely plant than even to see pictures or to merely be told of the process. We watched an avocado seed soak in a jar, sprout a root and stem system, and become a plant in our yard. Our children learned by observing this fascinating creative process, not just by our telling them.

In the busy world of adult activities parents are easily tempted to substitute words for experiences when relating to the child. Most of us need to be more alert to opportunities which provide firsthand experiences for our children.

Seven-year-old Todd asks dad to set up the electric train set. Wisely dad suggests that they do it together. In the process father and son share together, but Todd is also gaining firsthand experience in constructing the complicated train track. Through this guided experience Todd is learning, growing, developing.

Children need to do for themselves. The parent who recognizes the immense value of the child's personal experience will seek opportunities to guide him into profitable learning experiences. A rule I try to apply is to never do for my child what he can more profitably do for himself. This practical guideline helps me refocus my concern from the expediency of getting the task accomplished to making it an enriching experience for my child. I've found myself working on a project when Joel would come along and say, "Dad, can I try it?" My initial reaction tends to be "No, you're too young." But often I realize that this is a valuable learning experience for him, so I let him participate.

Joel is making a string art gift for his teacher. A couple of times I have been tempted to step in to sand the wood base or complete one of the steps in the process. However, I held back and let him do the work because it will be more profitable to him if he is able to complete the project.

Of course there are occasions when time is an important factor and a task must be completed quickly. Jody wants to button her coat herself but we are already late. Generally, however, abundant opportunities arise to allow the child firsthand experiences in learning.

If our children are to learn from firsthand experience, we must place greater value on the experience than on perishable materials or objects. As I am writing this chapter, Jody, my six-year-old daughter, is outside playing with her friend, Dawn. She has discovered some shelf boards in the garage and I overhear her telling Dawn that they are making a jail! Winnie, my wife, tells Jody that she must not play with daddy's good boards. However, as I peer out the window I see that a valuable learning experience is underway as the children try to create a simple structure. The lumber is likely put to its best use.

I mention this illustration to underscore how easy it is to deny our child the use of materials which can enrich his personal learning. Many such events in everyday family life can readily be transformed into valuable learning experiences if we can gain the proper perspective.

Your Child Learns from Vicarious Experiences

Vicarious experiences are those which someone else has had that are shared with the child. You may be able to recall some book you read as a youngster which impressed you deeply. Perhaps some fictional character helped you gain new insight into what loneliness or heartbreak is. Some of the most fruitful vicarious experiences are contained in the books children read. You will want to spend time regularly with your child reading stories which contain helpful examples of right conduct, character and attitudes. Even those stories which involve failure can be used, when followed by informal conversation exploring why the failure occurred, or a better course of action.

Inviting people into your home who are experiencing a rich, full life can provide vicarious experiences for your child. Our family remembers when John—a college student majoring in biology—came to our house one evening and brought slides of reptiles he has studied in their natural habitat. The children were fascinated by God's creativeness as John explained many unique aspects of their development. This has led our son Joel into a deeper interest in studying and observing reptiles. John's interest spurred an interest in Joel.

Children's lives are enriched significantly when we give opportunity for them to learn from different generations, different cultures, and different special interests. I value the stories my granddad told me when I was a boy, of his experiences working in the train yards. In other families children have gained a new perspective on the life of a missionary because the parents invited one to spend a week with the family.

My children can also learn from the experiences of my life if these experiences are translated into meaningful terms. Often at bedtime I tell my children an event from my childhood—giving myself another name to heighten the mystery. Thus, I can share with my children the successes and failures, the joys and the sorrows of my life in an intimate and enjoyable manner. In the process I enjoy a moment of closeness with my child as does he or she with me as he enjoys a vicarious experience from the life of someone dear to him.

Television provides a powerful vicarious experience for children. While much television programming is destructive, carefully chosen programs can be profitably used. Our family enjoys watching "Little House on the Prairie." Frequently we discuss some issue which the program portrays. Generally television is a problem because it is seldom well supervised, leaving viewing to the child's personal choice.

Your Child Learns from Asking Questions

Joel and I were on our way to the store one morning. He asked me, "Dad, why can the birds sit on the electric wire and not get shocked? If we were to do it we would get shocked."

After we had discussed the question briefly, he said, "Would you get shocked if you touched the wire holding onto the pole?" More discussion! Finally he was satisfied with the information that he had received. This was an important question and learning time for Joel. Questions and learning are partners. From early childhood through elementary school the healthy child demonstrates a consistent curiosity about almost all facets of life. When an adult is nearby, the curiosity can be satisfied by asking this "all knowing" (from the child's point of view) person to explain the phenomenon.

Too frequently, however, the parent is too busy or too impatient to share the learning experience with the child. Sometimes the adult turns off the child's question without realizing it. For example, I'm reading the newspaper and one of my children approaches me with a question. My first interest is the newspaper; my second interest is the question. Thus, the spirit of my answer is communicated to my child and he is discouraged from pursuing that question or others at a later date. If we can develop a sensitivity to lay aside the newspaper, book or "important" business to talk seriously with the child, we will be encouraging the spirit of learning in him.

Not only do our children learn from the questions they ask but also from the questions we ask. Frequently we realize that our child has become interested in some new object or phenomenon. Our skillful use of questions can aid the child in discovering why an object is designed the way it is, or how it operates.

Suppose you are looking at a picture book with a young child. You may ask such questions as, "What is the boy doing?" "What color is the dog?" "How many tricycles are on the lawn?" "Which girl is taller?" Such questions encourage even the young child to discriminate and define what he observes. It will encourage his looking more closely for details.

Even as your children grow older and are in elementary school, the thoughtful use of questions can challenge and direct their thinking. Use "how" and "why" questions that relate to values and attitudes: "Why do you think that Tony threw a stone through the window?" "Why do you want to be baptized?" "Why do you suppose the Good Samaritan stopped and helped an injured man?" "How could you show Mary that you are sorry about what happened to her?"

Most parents confess that it takes extra patience to answer the child's questions in a kind and helpful spirit. We also have to work diligently to regularly ask our children questions which stimulate their thought and excite discovery. It is well worth any extra effort expended to become more proficient in this area.

Your Child Learns from Play Experiences

God in His great wisdom planned that children make important discoveries about His world through play. Play is both remarkably simple and amazingly profound.

Children learn a significant part of their fundamental life skills through play activities. Their physical development is strengthened, refined and improved through climbing, crawling, swinging, running, throwing, etc. Their mental development progresses through stacking, manipulating and experimenting with objects. Their social development is enhanced as they learn to play together, share toys, follow rules of games, etc. Life-style values and attitudes are formulated through such actions as sharing, winning and losing in good spirit; and in working together with others to achieve a goal.

Parents can influence how profitable the child's play activities become. While we sometimes joke about "educational" toys, some toys do have greater value than others. Let me suggest the following guidelines for planning profitable play experiences:

1. Choose durable, safe toys and play equipment. Toys designed by reputable companies like Playskool and Creative Playthings are well constructed to take much punishment.

2. Choose toys with multiple use. For example, we purchased "Lego"[1]—a durable set of plastic building blocks for Joel—and he has spent countless hours constructing buildings, automobiles, unique designs, etc. Every time they are used something different can be constructed.

3. Purchase play objects for younger children which help them discriminate a variety of sizes, shapes, and colors, and textures. Toys which encourage the child to put different shapes through corresponding holes are excellent. Also, provide toys and experiences which allow the child to explore textures, tastes, smells, and sounds.

4. Avoid toys which tend to make the child a passive spectator. Many battery-operated playthings sold today are entertainment-oriented rather than growth-oriented.

5. Talk to other parents and find out what play equipment they have found profitable.

6. Make available "non-toy" equipment for your child. Pots and pans, pieces of wood, large appliance boxes, etc., will usually delight and pique the imagination of a child for a long time.

One day Amy and I were walking to the grocery store to purchase ice cream. On the way we saw a man who had placed two large planks on a concrete fence and then placed the other ends on a large barrel. The whole structure was in the form of a large triangle. Five pre-school children were having a delightful time "walking the plank" under his guidance. I was impressed by his thoughtfulness in constructing the walkway for the children, their obvious happiness in the activity, and the way they were sharpening their sense of balance. It impressed me as such an excellent illustration of how parents can plan for their children to play profitably.

Children are ready for different toys and experiences at different ages. The two-year-old may not have any interest in some toys; but when he is three he may spend much time with these same objects.

Every family needs to play together. Although some adults find it difficult to wholeheartedly enter into play with children, the value of wholesome family play in enriching family relationships far outweighs the discomfort. Again from my personal experience—I know that my relationship with my children has deepened through playing games, building with Lego blocks, or sledding in the snow.

Your Child Learns at His Own Speed and in His Own Way

After Joel had been a week in the first grade his teacher asked Winnie and me to come in for a conference. "Joel is not ready for first grade yet," she said. "He has more difficulty concentrating on a task because he is still young (he had entered as an early six-year-old). I recommend that you let him spend another year in kindergarten."

We took the teacher's counsel. Initially it was not easy. You know the feeling, "Our child cannot make it in the first grade." Yet once we realized that it was for Joel's benefit we knew that it was the right thing to do. Now, several years later Joel's school work is excellent and I'm certain he has prospered more than if he had had the frustration and struggle to keep up at the very start of his schooling.

A tendency exists today among some parents to push children too fast, before they are ready for certain learning experiences. I feel that this is especially true in spiritual matters. One school of thought is to "cram as much Bible into a child's head as you can when he is young because you may not have a chance later." Too often this results in a mass of confused, poorly taught Bible half-truths.

Here is a better way. First, trust God for the spiritual well-being of your child. Believe that He will bring the child to Himself in His time through the leading of the Holy Spirit. Then, make the most of sharing the reality of Christ in everyday living. If you believe that God designed the beauty of flowers then praise Him in a genuine spirit when you and your youngster are looking at them. If you are convinced that God answers prayer, allow your child to realize it as you earnestly pray in his presence. Point out to your child the ways that God answers your prayers. Third, when your child is still a preschooler share with him simple Bible stories which are written for little ones. Avoid many words beyond his comprehension. Avoid symbolism which confuses the child. I try to follow this guideline: As much as possible let everything stand for what it is.

Use questions wisely to discern what your child does and does not understand. Encourage him to share words, ideas or thoughts with which he is having difficulty. Listen to his questions. Recently one of the younger children asked if our kitten, Fluffy, could become a Christian. This question gave me valuable insight into where the child is in understanding spiritual concepts.

In summary, I want to stress that parents should not push. Provide opportunities—yes. Cooperate with the learning process—yes. But recognize that children differ. Allow each to proceed at his own pace.

PARENTS' PLAN FOR ACTION

One of the goals I suggested in the Introduction of this book was that Christian parents provide opportunities for their child to grow, to discover, to create. The following activities will help you achieve this goal in your home.

Where We Are Now

A. Evaluate your home as a learning environment by completing the following statements.
1. List books available to the child to look at and/or read (appropriate to his age level).
2. Identify what there is for him to see (pictures, objects, windows to look out, etc.).
3. What material is available for him to touch and manipulate of various sizes, textures and shapes?
4. What objects are there for him to climb on, in, under, or over?
5. Identify any expressions of God's creation in your home (flowers, plants, fish, pets, etc.).

6. What variety of sounds is the child exposed to? (records, radio, house noise, people's voices, animals, etc.).
B. Complete the following checklist to help you identify overlooked opportunities.

YES   NO

1. I use complete sentences more often than phrases or single words when speaking to my child.
2. I usually define, discuss, and illustrate new words or ideas to my child.
3. I take time to explain simple features of an object which are unknown to the child.
4. When I take my child to the store I take time to explain new items or new processes he is curious about.
5. I frequently sit down and look at/read books with my child.

What We Want to Do

Choose one of the following action plans to work on in the days ahead:
A. Using the checklist below, rate yourself as to the guidance you give your child in the following mediums of vicarious experiences. After completing the checklist, jot down specific ways you can more purposefully guide or control the experiences to which your child is exposed.

VICARIOUS EXPERIENCE	CONSISTENT GUIDANCE	OCCASIONAL GUIDANCE	NO GUIDANCE
Visitor in home			
Music (radio, records)			
Television			
Books			
Comics			
Magazines			
(Other)			

B. Plan a "field trip" with your child each week. The purpose is to spend quality time with him in which you can enrich his learning. Plan the trip according to his age. For example, if your child is a preschooler you might go to the children's petting zoo at the local zoo. While there you could identify a few animals and let your child feel their coats. Talk with him according to his ability to understand. Choose from the ideas below and plan a month's "field trips." (Be sure to put it on your calendar.)

1. Construction site
2. Farm
3. Airport
4. Factory tour
5. Museum
6. Ocean, lake, river
7. Hobby shop
8. Special interest store
9. Fire station
10. Walk in neighborhood
11. Botanical gardens
12. Trip to mountains
13. Toy shop
14. Overnight campout
15. Library

Footnote

1. Manufactured by Lego System A/S, Enfield, Conn., 06082. Available at most toy departments and stores.

Basic Family Goal 3

To Provide Opportunities to Grow, Discover, Create

7 How to Read to Your Child

As you read this chapter, you will discover ...
- the importance of reading to your child's intellectual development
- the importance of reading to your child's emotional development
- the importance of reading to your child's spiritual development
- how to read to your child
- what to read to your child

How to Read to Your Child

When our Jody was about two years old she would
sometimes disappear into her room, reappear with several books and begin to chant, "Read, Daddy, read," or,
"Read, Mommy, read." We did read to Jody because we
are convinced that young children quickly learn to enjoy books and develop good feelings about reading when
parents make reading aloud a happy time.

A respected Christian educator, Frank Gaebelein,
once stated, "The home is still the greatest educational

force, and parents who make reading attractive contribute immeasurably to their children's intellectual, emotional, and spiritual development. Forty-one years as a headmaster have convinced me that a genuinely educated person is one who knows how to read and who keeps on reading throughout his life."[1]

In fact, mothers and dads are generally the key to a child's interest and aptitude for reading. If he has had stories read to him, has had the fun of handling books on his own, chances are he has developed some kind of aptitude toward books and reading and will come to school anticipating the experience of learning to read. He has already discovered that reading is fun and that books are his friends.

On the other hand, if the child has had few good story times with his parents, has not learned to enjoy looking at books and has spent much time being entertained by TV, he may very well approach reading with disinterest and indifference.

Why Read to Your Child

Reading aloud to your child and enjoying books and stories together is more than just fun, for reading aloud provides benefits for you and your child. Unfortunately many parents have not realized this and have robbed both themselves and their child of rich experiences.

As you consider the following benefits of reading to or with your child, plan how you can claim each benefit for yourself and your child.

1. Reading Encourages a Healthy Parent-child Relationship

Reading provides a common ground where parent and child can join in the world of imagination, wonder and humor. Our family has enjoyed countless hours of good times reading stories together. If you as a parent will invest time in this activity you will likely find that this can be a rewarding and relaxing intimate experience with your child.

2. Reading Stimulates Intellectual Growth

Well-chosen books broaden a child's range of interests. He becomes acquainted with new, fascinating animals, with great and small wonders of God's creation and with the ways of people in other lands. Reading to a young child enriches his imagination—an integral force in fostering intellectual growth—and facilitates the development of the child's thought processes by increasing his vocabulary.

3. Reading Develops Language Skills

The parent who often reads to his child helps widen the child's selection of words and meanings, his ability to be increasingly precise, discriminating and verbally expressive. Even when the child does not understand the meaning of a word being read to him, he nevertheless is gaining skill in forming words and hearing sounds. Thus, reading is an excellent way to help the child to develop good language skills. The significance of reading to the young child is that it provides one of the powerful building blocks in the child's language development prior to the school years. Many school systems now provide rich language experiences for children under six so they can move ahead when they enter first grade.

4. Reading Communicates Healthy Attitudes, Ideals and Values

Books that we shared with our children in their early years have helped to teach them—reverence when praying. We enjoyed a little book called *Sh-h-h-h* by Mary LeBar on the subject of prayer. Another book by Dr. LeBar titled *Johnny's Cookies* was helpful in illustrating the concept of the joy in sharing. *Joe's Strong Legs*, also by Dr. LeBar, helped develop a sense of thankfulness for a healthy body, especially all the things strong legs help a child to do.[2] Just the other day I enjoyed stretching out on the living room floor and reading to my children Gilbert Beers' delightful little book titled *The Magic Merry-Go-Round*.[3] Skillfully woven into the fabric of this story is the important truth of boys and girls entering into a personal relationship with Jesus Christ.

5. Reading Creates Love for Books
Through those relaxed reading experiences an enduring thirst for good books can be created. Instilling a love for good books in your child will bring rich dividends which will last a lifetime.

6. Reading Prepares the Child for Bible-reading Experiences
When children came into our marriage, Winnie and I desired that they would grow to love, read and obey the Word of God. Their early enjoyment of the reading process was one step in that direction. Today we look back over the few years and recognize that one of the chief means for encouraging in our children positive attitudes toward the Bible has been our earlier efforts to instill a spirit of enjoyment toward books in general. In a small way we are beginning to see the dividends of this labor.

The summer when Amy was nine years old I encouraged her to set aside time daily to read through the New Testament. (We had provided her with a reliable children's version.) In time I realized that this was an unrealistic goal. She did, however, read through each of the Gospels and the book of Acts. This was completed with a minimum of reminding on our part for she had planned the reading into her day's activities. This summer she has completed the books of Ruth and Esther and is now reading in the book of Proverbs.

Two instances in my own experience underscore the great need for Christian parents to create in their children an interest in reading. The first instance was several years ago when I was involved in a youth ministry in a local church. I noticed that many young people had little interest in reading their Bibles. Often I found that these teenagers had not been motivated to read as youngsters and/or had experienced difficulty in the skill of reading.

More recently I attempted to provide opportunities for second- and third-graders to spend time reading Christian books during a portion of the Primary Church hour. I felt that many children would look forward to this opportunity. To my dismay, I discovered that very few had any interest in reading.

Our culture provides so many visual forms of entertainment by way of TV that many children have little desire to explore the fascinating world of books. Unless parents work diligently to stimulate an appetite for good books and magazines, children are denied an exciting world of enrichment and imagination. In the parental responsibility to control our children's (and our own) television viewing, it is a sound principle to place something intriguing and fun in its place—and good books offer just that.

How to Read to Your Child

The question sounds remarkably naive. "You've gotta be kidding! I know how to read to my child. Any person who knows how to read can read to a little kid!"

But wait a minute! To read effectively to your child involves more skill than the processes of pronouncing words correctly, or reading a sentence smoothly. These skills provide a necessary start, but much more can be added to make reading to your child an enriching experience, and delightful to parent and child alike. Let me recommend a few simple guidelines for developing happy and effective reading times with your child:

1. Begin early. If you are to cope adequately with the challenge of reading to your child you must begin early. I would stress that the time to begin reading to your child is when he is an infant—before he can speak or understand. Of course, "reading" to the child at this age is a brief, informal experience of looking at pictures and attaching words to them. However, this process of looking at familiar pictures in books and hearing word-sounds attached to them is an intellectually stimulating experience for the child. In addition, the very act of your doing it with your child suggests that it is important. The brief moments you spend with the infant leafing through a simple picture book is a foundational experience with much value. Nancy Larrick, in her guide to children's literature, emphasizes this point in her statement, "A child's aptitude for reading is determined long before he enters first grade. Indeed, some specialists say there is little that the primary-grade teacher can do to help a child overcome the crippling effect of language starvation in his first five years."[4]

2. Plan when to read. Begin by mentally evaluating your time schedule. When is the best time for you to read to the child? When is the best time for the child? By all means take advantage of spontaneous situations when the child asks to be read to, or when you think of it. But making reading an ongoing, fruitful learning

105

experience requires sensitivity on your part as to the best time to read.

Let me give you a "for instance." Much of the day at our house is filled with busy activity. We usually cannot read to the children at just anytime. We have, however, found a convenient, effective time to read to Jody. Because she is still taking a nap she stays up a half hour to an hour later than the other children. The house is quiet, we are more relaxed. This is an excellent occasion to read to Jody. She anticipates it and we as parents can give ourselves completely to the task.

You must find the time spots in your day which are most suitable for you and your child. Once you have discovered this time endeavor to work that in as a regular part of your schedule. Plan for that event with your child.

3. Plan what to read. A significant number of books written for children are of poor quality. To spend time reading them represents poor use of your time—as well as the child's. It really is not difficult to discover the better books to choose from. Let me suggest several sources which can assist you: *Honey For a Child's Heart* by Gladys Hunt (Zondervan) is probably the best book available from a Christian perspective which suggests both Christian and non-Christian books for children. *A Parent's Guide to Children's Reading* by Nancy Larrick (Doubleday), and *Reading with Your Child Through Age 5* (Child Study Press) are also helpful sources to guide you in the choice of children's books. Creating a desire for good books before the child is able to read the Bible is an excellent means of creating a desire later for reading the Word of God.

As children begin to read, consider enrolling them in a children's book-of-the-month club. We find the selections are usually appropriate and give a child the joyful experience of receiving his own book and beginning to build his own library. Having some books of his own also enhances reading in the mind of the child.

What to Read to Your Child

According to Gladys Hunt, "A good book is a magic gateway into a wider world of wonder, of beauty, of delight and adventure."[5]

Several guidelines are helpful in planning what to read to your child. First, read stories children enjoy. Basically, children find satisfaction in stories with which they can identify. The young child discovers pleasure in stories about other young children, familiar animals and familiar situations. He enjoys imaginary situations if they are not fearful. He delights in stories that are mostly pictures. The younger child requires stories that use simple, understandable (or easily explainable) words and short sentences. As the child grows, his range of interests expands and so he enjoys hearing stories relevant to his widening range of interests.

Second, read children's stories with action. Children are action-oriented. They want to hear about something happening.

Third, choose stories with positive value. What does the story teach? (Later, I will suggest conversation related to the story. If the account has an attitude, value or ideal embodied in it, informal conversation will reinforce the concept portrayed.)

Fourth, select and read a rich variety of books to your child: humorous, sad, adventuresome, true-life, stories of great persons. When your child becomes school age, read open-ended stories; these are stories that present a problem or situation, then allow parent and child to suggest possible solutions. These stories are excellent for discussing and thinking through values.

Tips for Enjoying a Book with Your Child

1. Read creatively. Like many other family experiences parents largely determine whether reading becomes a boring routine or a refreshing new occasion.

2. Learn to read expressively. Put feeling into words. Attempt to project yourself into the story. Feel what those in the story feel. When it says, "Jack cried out in anger!" express what Jack says with a tone of anger.

3. Read the same book in a variety of ways. Young children thrive on repetition; thus, they ask for familiar books to be read again and again. To take advantage of this, the following plan may be useful. The first time you share the book with the child let him leaf through it with you. Talk about it; answer his questions of curiosity. The second time through "read" the story by talking about the pictures. This helps the child to think through the story visually. Three- to five-year-olds enjoy looking through the pictures of a book, identifying less significant elements. You may say, "Where's the caterpillar?" or "Where's the bird?" to challenge the child to look closely and become more discriminating in what he sees. If you read the story immediately the child will be looking at the pictures and will hear less of the story. The third time through read the text of the story. The fourth time ask the child to retell the story to you. You may let him tell it from the pictures.

We use variations on these ideas. For example, when the child has become quite familiar with the story, as we read it we leave out a word and let the child "fill in the blank." Of course the word should be an important word such as an action word or a person's name. Recently I read a story to Jody about a frog and a toad. She had to fill in the missing word, whether it was frog or toad. The event became very humorous as she would get "frog" in "toad's" place, and vice versa.

4. Use creative follow-up. For example, children enjoy drawing a picture of their favorite part of the story. Another follow-up activity is simply to allow each person to ask another family member a question about the story as a playful test of memory. This process calls for attentiveness from all, as well as a playful, enjoyable experience for the family.

Reading with our children provides us with good value-related situations for discussion. This is especially true when children come of school age. Not long ago we were reading a C.S. Lewis classic, *The Lion, the Witch, and the Wardrobe* (Macmillan). In the story, Edward lies to his brother and sister about Lucy, his other sister. One could feel the anguish Lucy felt when in Edward's lying she appeared to be untruthful. We talked together about what others feel when we are not honest. Edward's lie in the story helped our family appreciate the value of truth.

You can make a story even more valuable by asking questions. Parents can build skill in the use of questions. With the young child ask factual questions: "What is that?" "What color is the flower in the picture?" "Which animal jumped over the moon?"

As the child develops, a slightly more thoughtful question can be injected. "How would you do that?" "When did something like that happen to you?" When the child enters school, parents can move to an even deeper level of thinking. "Why did Alex feel frightened?" "What caused the man to become angry?" "How did the woman at the well feel when Jesus asked a favor?"

Well chosen, clearly stated questions have great power to provoke thought, to direct thought, and to apply truth to life. Effective questions allow the parent to guide the child's thinking processes without saying "I told you so!" or "Let me tell you about it" which take away from the child the joy of personal discovery.

5. Read for fun and humor. Parents and their children should experience many delightful hours of fascinating entertainment as they read aloud. Several years ago we were moving from Kentucky to California. Just prior to the move, I chanced to purchase the ridiculously humorous book, *Pippi Longstockings*, by Astrid Lindgren (Viking). As we traveled across country the entire family looked forward to the restful evening at a motel when we would laugh together at the antics of Pippi. We would test each other's memory to see if we could pronounce her entire name. We still have fond memories of our zany friend Pippi. She made her contribution to our lives.

Read to learn through vicarious experiences. Many life occurrences are intensified when we read of similar happenings in a story, whether fact or fiction. Frequently we perceive more deeply how others feel or think as we read an account from that person's point of view. We recently read together the story of *Adopted Jane* by H.R. Daringer (Scholastic). All of us understood more what it would be like to live in an institution without a mother or dad to care for us personally, without a room of our own. Many enlightening thoughts occurred in the minds of all of our family members which we could not have experienced personally.

Because books contain the power to provide vicarious experiences, the alert parent will try to become knowledgeable about quality books. He will explore those presenting a wide range of experiences and points in history. Books and stories help the parent open doors to exciting worthwhile experiences for his children's growth. As Gladys Hunt says, "Any good book can be used by God in a child's development, for a good book has genuine spiritual substance, not just intellectual enjoyment."[6]

One point of caution. If the point of identification is too wide between the child and the person in the story, the value of the book will probably be less. For example, a child can more likely identify with a story of another child than a story about an adult.

Make stories and books an important part of your family life. Become proficient at discovering those books which will genuinely enrich each member of the family. When your children are young stimulate an appetite for books; when they become older guide them into wholesome reading by example and instruction.

PARENTS' PLAN FOR ACTION
You can be the key in your child's life to unlock the door to joy and discovery through reading. Plan now how you can help him or her discover that reading really is fun and that books are good friends.

Where We Are Now
The statements listed below may help you evaluate your own attitude toward reading. Check whether or not these statements are true in your home.

	YES	NO
1. I enjoy reading books and magazines.		
2. I read poorly.		
3. I am too busy to read to my child.		
4. I leave it to my spouse to read to the children.		
5. We have a good variety of books available, appropriate for my child's		

age, interest, and reading   YES   NO
ability.

6. In a positive (non-nag-
   ging) way I encourage
   and guide my child's
   reading habits.

7. I read to my child daily.

Your responses to the above statements may suggest areas you would like to work on.

I would suggest that you plan a trip to your public library.

What We Want to Do

Circle the items below which you plan to work on this week.

1. Take your child on a tour of the children's book section in the local library.

2. Visit a local Christian bookstore and review the children's books they stock.

3. Develop a schedule for the coming week to begin reading with your child.

4. Read *Honey for a Child's Heart*, Gladys Hunt (Zondervan), to enrich your understanding of children's literature.

Footnotes

1. Gladys Hunt, *Honey for a Child's Heart* (Grand Rapids: Zondervan, 1969), p. 2 (Introduction).
2. Mary LeBar, *Sh-h-h-h* (Wheaton: Scripture Press, 1950).
   _____, *Johnny's Cookies* (Wheaton: Scripture Press, 1951).
   _____, *Joe's Strong Legs* (Wheaton: Scripture Press, 1951).
3. Gilbert Beers, *The Magic Merry-Go-Round* (Chicago: Moody Press, 1973).
4. Nancy Larrick, *A Parent's Guide to Children's Reading* (New York: Doubleday, 1975, 4th revised edition), p. 25.
5. Gladys Hunt, *Honey for a Child's Heart* (Grand Rapids: Zondervan, 1969), p.14.
6. *Ibid.*, p. 18.

Basic Family Goal 4

To Discover and Work Toward God's Will and Purpose for Our Family

8 How to Communicate a Life-Style (Values)

As you read this chapter, you will discover . . .
- the meaning of "values"
- how to identify your own values
- how to deal with the question "Should we teach values?"
- seven values worth living by

How to Communicate a Life-Style (Values)

A troubled young man entered my office and sat down. He was bothered by family problems that plagued members of his church. During the course of our conversation I asked him what his pastor was doing to help families with problems. "Not long ago he had a series of messages on the Christian home," he replied. "The trouble is, the pastor is the worst violator of the principles he preaches about. He neglects his family as much as the rest. I wish he would set a better example!"

114

This pastor is an example of a person who says he believes certain principles are important but in reality lives by a different set of values. His professed belief is inconsistent with the values his life expresses. He is communicating his real values through his life-style, not by what he said he believed!

What Do We Mean by Values?

Most of us are guilty of using words which we have not clearly defined in our mind. While it may often cause us no apparent problem, sometimes it leads to a vagueness of communication or purpose. This is especially true when we use the word "values." We may feel that something is truly important but not actually comprehend its meaning for our own life. When asked to state our values we are frequently at a loss to do so.

For me a value is a principle which I cherish or prize highly enough that I practice it in my life. Valuing suggests that I hold something in esteem, place great worth upon it, or cherish it dearly. Values are frequently stated as ideals or principles by which we measure both our own actions and those of others. Hopefully, these ideals are powerful enough to give purpose and direction in living. My values signify what I feel is important in life. My values become my standard by which I choose and measure goals, the worth of an activity or object, or desire.

Should We Teach Values?

One issue which the Christian parent must resolve is whether or not he should conscientiously and deliberately teach values. This question can be answered in at least four ways.

Someone may say, "Kids are too young to be taught values. Wait until they are teenagers and can think more intelligently." From this point of view we avoid any reference of value-issues lest we confuse the child.

A second answer is, "Parents should not impose their values on their children, who should have the privilege of choosing their own. Be neutral and just help the child clarify his own value system."

A third response is, "Live by your own values and your child will automatically adopt those as his own." To follow this course of action I will not discuss my values with my children though I will seek to be a good example and illustrate wholesome values by my life.

I believe that the biblical response to this question gives a fourth option. The Scriptures (particularly Deut. 6:4-9, *TLB*) indicate that we should *incarnate* values ("these words shall be on your heart") and also *instruct* ("you shall teach them diligently") our children in basic Christian values. This passage from Deuteronomy also suggests that values may be visualized ("write them on the doorposts") in the home so that the child sees them in visual form.

Actually none of the first three options to the question are realistic, for we are constantly teaching values whether we acknowledge it or not. For example, Amy and Jill frequently have their bedroom door closed when they are reading or playing in their room. When I knock on the door and do not "barge in," I acknowledge the value of respecting personal privacy. I feel strongly about the value of privacy, but unless I identify this value by consistently demonstrating it in everyday situations with the children, I am not living a life-style which communicates this particular value.

Identifying Cherished Values

Because my values represent those principles which I cherish or highly prize, I should be able to identify them.

Otherwise I may not conscientiously seek to pass them on to my children. In the following pages I would like to identify seven values which are important to my wife and me and suggest how we are endeavoring to teach them to our children. These values are not given in any order of importance.

1. Knowing and having personal fellowship with God is of vital importance to us. Ultimately whatever is accomplished which is of lasting value will result from our love for and obedience to Jesus Christ. We believe that whatever else we may do in life will be of little consequence if we do not walk in obedience with the Lord.

The importance of our relationship to our heavenly Father manifests itself to the children in numerous ways. They observe us studying His Word. When Winnie or I sense that the Lord is speaking to us about some matter, we may share this informally with one or all of the children. Our individual and family prayer times testify to our desire to be in an intimate relationship with Him.

Recently we were confronted with a very important decision as to whether the Lord was leading us to move to Phoenix, Arizona, to become involved in a new ministry. It would require selling our house, leaving behind many intimate friendships, and relocating in a new community. None of us relished the idea of severing our intensely satisfying relationships. However, as we shared the situation with the children we sought to communicate our earnest desire to be where the Lord wanted us to be. Our wanting His plan for our life could be felt by our children.

I recall a fellow student relating an incident to me when I was in college which further illustrates what I am saying. This student, whose parents were home missionaries, shared how that many times needs would occur in the family. For example, a situation would arise which required additional finances to meet a pressing need. In these circumstances she would see her parents pray in earnest dependence and faith to their heavenly Father. In those incidents she saw the evidence of her parents' faith and God's provision. "As a result," she continued, "when I reach into my mailbox now and find a bill to be paid, I find great confidence in my parents' Provider who has become my Provider."

Winnie and I earnestly desire above all else that our children place the highest value upon their personal relationship to the living God. We have sought to lead each one to a personal relationship to Jesus Christ so that they might know Him personally. We pray with them daily to help them develop a personal fellowship with the Lord and to share our relationship with Him, as an example. We have encouraged them to build their own relationship with Him while they are young (Eccles. 12:1).

2. Showing care and concern for others is a second value which we seek to demonstrate and encourage in our children. If children do not grow to care about others and show this care in specific actions they may develop into basically selfish persons. I cherish the wish that my children become persons who care deeply about others and act with compassion.

Recently a seminary student related his experience of learning from his parents to care for others. I asked him how his parents taught him. He said that they expressed this concern by inviting persons into their home for meals, taking clothing to families in distress, assisting persons who had lost a family member by death. He consistently observed his mom and dad coming to the aid of persons in distress. Now he has chosen that as one of his own values.

Being concerned about others is most likely to be demonstrated first toward family members. Our attitude of caring about the child or other family member who has been injured does not go unnoticed. Or, when a child feels discouraged by a broken friendship, an overload of homework, or some disappointment, our children see how we respond in demonstrating loving concern and understanding for another family member frustrated by these situations. We demonstrate that caring about what happens to others and how they feel is important to us.

Not long ago Joel found a lizard behind one of the Sunday School buildings at church. He brought it home, planning to give it to his buddy who collects such creatures. That afternoon while showing it to another friend the lizard made a fast move and got away. Joel came home, heartbroken, with tears in his eyes. Winnie and I understood that this was a very real disappointment to Joel who had planned to give the lizard as a special gift. By our sincere example the other family members could empathize with Joel.

Caring is reflected in the family members' affection for each other. Men who believe that they should show a tough, unemotional image to their children deceive themselves. Jesus Christ was superb in His deep loving care for persons in distress. I am reminded of His sincere compassion for Mary and Martha as they grieved over the death of their brother Lazarus. He was moved with emotion for their loss and the Bible records that He wept. Even so, mothers and dads who take their children up in their arms and express warm affection are laying the foundation for compassion in their children.

I have been seriously considering building a wooden picture of a flower with individual petals that represent each family member. The petals would be removable. To one side I would place a couple of pegs. When a family member felt discouraged, hurt or in need of comfort he could take his "petal" from the flower and place it on one of the pegs. This would signal family members that someone was hurting. If the person wanted someone special to share the problem he would take that person's "petal" off the flower and place it on the peg beside his own.

Someone may say, "Such things are not necessary. We should be naturally sensitive to family needs." My response is that in today's busy schedule we sometimes need cues to assist us in reaching out to show compassion. Anyway, I think I'll build the flower picture!

Opportunities to show this value of caring about others outside the family abound. For example, we recently received a letter from World Vision which related the distress of millions in India. My heart was touched by the plight of my fellowman. I shared the letter with the children and we discussed what we could do to assist. We decided that we could open our "piggy banks" and send a love gift. A bit later that evening one of the children came with a dollar bill and said, "I'm sure that I can get along without this. Put it toward the love gift." I was grateful for that personal expression of love.

3. Demonstrating respect for others is the third value high on our family's list. It is vitally important to us as parents that our children come to respect others and recognize this as an essential life value. This value, too, can be most powerfully learned in the home and begins with the respect manifested in the husband-wife relationship. If children observe one spouse verbally attack, criticize, or ridicule the other spouse they are likely to think that this is the appropriate way to respond. The child will probably incorporate such behavior into his life-style.

Parents also demonstrate respect for others in their attitudes toward their children. When a mother yells at her son, "You stupid dummy, why'd you do that?" she is encouraging a brother or sister to think of the child in a disrespectful manner. Winnie and I find that this value is regularly "on the line" as we confront problem situations that tax our patience within the home. We are learning that even in everyday situations such as Annette's spilling her milk, Joel and Jill getting into a scrap, or Amy and her mother differing over a dress style, we do have the options to demonstrate either patience and respect, or annoyance and disrespect by the way we respond to these situations. How easily we forget that "love is patient" (1 Cor. 13:4).

One specific way that we have sought to teach respect for family members is by memorizing and discussing appropriate verses of Scripture which relate to this area. For example, the passage in Ephesians 4:25-32 has been useful for us as a family as a model of courtesy and respect. Probably of all the values we seek to demonstrate and impart to our children, this one has required the most time and effort because of children's basic difficulty in learning to move from self-centeredness to concern for the feelings of others.

4. Prizing the uniqueness of ourself and our life potential is a fourth value we are concerned about living and passing on. In a culture which promotes an intense peer-group pressure, individuals need to value their own God-given uniqueness. Each life has distinctive potential which finds fulfillment in the plan which God has for each of us.

Frequently so-called "Christian standards" force believers into a subtle, stereotyped Christianity which stifles creativity and diminishes the beauty of each life reflecting in its own special way, the living Christ. As children in God's family we should prize the uniqueness and giftedness of our life and teach our children this value too.

Another dimension of this concept focuses on encouraging each child to recognize and value the potential of his life when it is submitted joyfully to God to be a source of great blessing. I desire that each of our children sense how fully the giftedness of his life can be used, for no person's life is insignificant in the plan of God.

One night we invited a number of seminary students and their wives to our home. During the evening two couples were playing the Ungame with Joel. One lady asked Joel, "What important thing have you learned from your dad?" Joel responded, "I've learned that I'm a good helper." He answered in this way because of the numerous times that I've complimented him for his willingness to use his energy to assist me. He sees himself as one who can use his life to be a blessing to others.

As parents we can encourage in various ways living out this value of God-given uniqueness in our children's lives. At our house it means not comparing one child with another. It means not requiring Jody to fit the mold of Amy's life. It means teaching Jill that the uniqueness of herself is something special. By helping each of them to recognize their individual uniqueness, we are helping them to expect and accept differences. One excels in one area whereas another excels in another area.

Also, when we sense an area of uniqueness we want to consider its potential for good and encourage the child to develop that area of his life. Our Amy, for example, enjoys being quiet and contemplative. This can be a lovely quality leading to a deepening sensitivity to life. At the same time our Jody's extroverted and expressive ways are equally valued and enriching qualities which she is learning to use with proper courtesy.

5. Cherishing a life of honesty and integrity has been another value we seek to uphold and encourage in our children. Nationally we have undergone much public disgrace as we discovered dishonesty among our leadership in such situations as "Watergate" and other more recent incidents. Sometimes children become disillusioned growing up in a society which tolerates double standards. However, if parents are consistent in their own life practices and take time to patiently clarify this value of integrity, their children can usually weather the storm.

Helping the child see a long-range perspective on honesty is an important aspect of teaching this value. From a child's limited perspective it may appear that "crime does pay." Parents must help put such issues in a biblical perspective with awareness of ultimate accountability of every life before God.

When the children are old enough to grasp it, a family Bible study of Psalm 73 can help children recognize that ultimately "crime doesn't pay." This psalm expresses the godly writer's confusion when he saw the ungodly prosper. He even became envious of the wicked (v. 3). He observed persons violate principles of right, and even mock God. As he wrestled with the seeming injustice, he says, "Surely in vain I have kept my heart pure, washed my hands in innocence" (v. 13). However, he finds a meaningful answer when he sees such behavior from God's perspective. The ungodly's accountability before God is a living reality. "How they are destroyed in a moment!" (v. 19).

We have sought to promote honesty as a personal and family value in several ways. First, Winnie and I endeavor to make it the practice of our own life. Second, we have placed a high premium on honesty in our children's lives. We have sought to underscore the long-range effects of dishonesty. Third, we have sought to use stories and life incidents which exalt truthfulness as a positive virtue.

6. Trusting in the Lord for all our life needs is a sixth value of importance to us. It is a dimension of our family life-style which we deeply cherish for our children. Holding to this value brings security and peace to mind and heart. Depending for one's sufficiency in himself, in others or in material resources demonstrates a life value which will ultimately be disappointing.

Perhaps more than any other value, our children need to see that trusting the Lord is an integral part of their parents' lives. The parents' deep and abiding confidence in the heavenly Father in the midst of difficult or seemingly impossible circumstances can make a lasting impression on the youngster.

I recall a time when Joel fractured a bone on the side of his head. The accident left him unable to speak properly or walk. We did not know what the long-term result would be, but we trusted God for the outcome, whatever it was. In this we were saying, "God is reliable. You can depend on Him."

By contrast, when mom or dad is fearful in many situations, he or she thereby discredits an all-powerful God. When we say that we are trusting in God but worry and feverishly seek every human way out, our children have a right to doubt the value of trusting in God for every life need. Once when I worked as a night clerk at a motel I was held up by a robber. I would like to say that I was not fearful and even told the man about Jesus Christ. As it actually happened, I had to tell my children how frightened I was during the event.

7. Assuming personal responsibility is the seventh value to be considered here. One reason this is an impor-

tant value is that it is a mark of a growing person. When one is able and willing to assume personal responsibility in one or more areas of life, he is ready to apply constructive measures to remedy a situation, rather than helplessly gripe and complain.

Even when our children were quite young we began to instill the value of assuming personal responsibility. We began a step at a time to help each child learn to dress himself and care for his personal hygiene, to make his own bed and care for his room and to share in other household responsibilities, insofar as he is able. This value of personal responsibilities is not limited to its development by means of these everyday tasks of living but should also be developed in matters of problem resolution, such as a child's learning to accept responsibility for solutions to disagreements.

I asked my wife, Winnie, if she remembered her parents teaching her to assume personal responsibility. With a laugh she mused, "Yes, but in a negative situation. I was to play in the school band on Saturday. However, I 'fiddled' around with housework I was asked to do. When it came time to leave for school my work was not done. I watched the school bus drive past my house—without me. Believe me, I learned to be responsible!"

A distinguishing mark of competent leadership is the ability to assume personal responsibility. Some individuals will do a task when instructed to do so and resist taking responsibility for anything but what is specifically assigned. Others see a need or problem involved which they recognize and take the responsibility without waiting to be told. They step in to help correct the matter. This second illustration marks the characteristic of the individual who is able to assume personal responsibility.

Communicating a Life-style

As I consider the values outlined above I am again impressed with how important it is that these values be taught—not left to chance. We must plan to teach. Such values must be taught both by life models and instruction. The teaching must be based on love rather than compulsion so that the learners may grow in the heart, not just the head.

Let's face it. Merely cramming "dos" and "don'ts" into our child's head won't do it. We have to begin by facing and answering some basic questions within ourselves. What values do I claim? Are they evident as an integral part of my everyday life? Do I seek to pass them on to my children in a loving, nurturing manner? The challenge of living and communicating a Christian lifestyle is a big challenge! You may choose to accept this personal responsibility and depend on God's promise of His forever family—"If you want to know what God wants you to do, ask him, and he will gladly tell you, for he is always ready to give a bountiful supply of wisdom to all who ask him" (Jas. 1:5, *TLB*).

(The concluding chapter, "How to Build Christian Character," discusses key principles involved in communicating values to your children.)

PARENTS' PLAN FOR ACTION

In this chapter I have been sharing with you values which my wife and I are seeking to instill into the lives of our children. Now I ask you to think and act upon this information as it relates to your family.

Where We Are Now

I suggest that you begin by marking on a piece of paper four columns. (See sketch.) Begin by identifying in the first column the values you want to impart to your own children. Then jot down why each value you listed is important, where you learned it (its source) and what the value will do for your children. See the following sample list for specific examples:

Values We Want to Communicate to Our Children		
Value we want to teach	Where we learned it	What we want it to do for our child
1. Keep promises	Biblical Concept	Develop respect and responsibility toward others
2. Share in household tasks as able	my parents	Develop family unity and personal responsibility

What We Want to Do

After you have identified the values you believe are important in God's plan for you and your children, choose one of these values you have identified to begin working on with your children and list three specific ways that you can teach that value by modeling it in your life and/or by your instruction.

Each week take time to pray earnestly as parents together about what and how you are communicating the value you have decided to teach. Gradually add the other values—a step at a time—until you are simultaneously communicating all the values you believe are important for your family.

Basic Family Goal 4

**To Discover and Work Toward God's Will
and Purpose for Our Family**

9 How to Build Christian Character

As you read this chapter, you will discover . . .
- ways to communicate values to your children
- ways to help your child internalize values
- characteristics of family life instrumental in developing wholesome values
- methods of integrating the processes of modeling, instruction and internalizing

How to Build
Christian Character

In foregoing chapters we have identified key Christian values that we want our children to adopt. Now the question is: How can we guide our children toward these values? How can we encourage our children to make these values a part of their lives?

Ways to Communicate Values to Your Child

There are three basic processes by which parents communicate values to their child—modeling, instructing and internalizing.

1. Modeling: I Am Doing It Because I See You Do It

You laugh. And your child laughs with you.

You cuddle your youngster. And he snuggles close.

You shout in anger. And your child shouts back.

The powerful process of modeling is at work as your child patterns his behavior on the behavior he sees and lives with. No doubt you have read the classic "Parent's Creed" written by Dorothy Law Nolte that gives examples of the modeling principle:

> If a child lives with criticism,
>   he learns to condemn . . .
> If a child lives with hostility,
>   he learns to fight . . .
> If a child lives with tolerance,
>   he learns to be patient . . .
> If a child lives with encouragement,
>   he learns confidence . . .
> If a child lives with praise,
>   he learns to appreciate . . .
> If a child lives with fairness,
>   he learns justice.[1]

Yes, guiding your child to accept values you consider important begins with your living out those values in your everyday life. What you do shows your child how to act, how to feel, how to cope with life.

God's Word underlines the importance of modeling in Deuteronomy 6:4-9 when God instructs the parent to "love the Lord your God with all your heart and with all your soul and with all your might." From this Scripture, the Christian parent discovers that he is to love God with his whole person—heart, soul, strength, so that his life can be a living demonstration of his faith and obedience to God.

What really counts when it comes to influencing your

children toward choosing a Christian life-style, is what they see in your life. Parents are guiding their child by modeling when, for instance, the youngster senses that dad loves God, talks about Him and talks to Him; and when the child tells a friend, "My mom really knows that Jesus is always with her."

The modeling process is an essential part of a parent's God-given privilege and responsibility for teaching the child in everyday situations.

Before our youngest child, Annette, was two years old we knew she could understand very little about the importance of love or showing love to one another. Our talking to her about this abstract concept of love was far beyond her understanding. Yet as we listened to Annette, kissed her, held her and helped her feel happy and safe, we did teach her much about love. Her loving response to us showed us how much she was learning about feeling and showing love.

The first year of a child's life is a time of key importance for modeling values for your child. In fact, the noted psychologist, Erik Erikson, holds that the infant develops his basic attitude toward trusting people during the first eighteen months of his life![2]

The importance of modeling is demonstrated many places in the Bible. One of the New Testament instances is Paul's reference to the young man Timothy, whose mother and grandmother he mentions as his first spiritual models. (See 2 Tim. 1:5.) Scripture also gives other examples of the modeling principle—sometimes in reverse. For example, a graphic picture of deceit is seen in Jacob's life. Jacob patterned his action after the deceit in his father's life just as Jacob's sons followed his example.

In his book, *You, the Parent,* Larry Richards points out that modeling " . . . is a process that focuses on what we *are*, not what we *say*. I may say to my son 'I value honesty, and want you to admit when you have done something wrong.' But if he sees me attempting to excuse my own errors rather than honestly facing and admitting them, he will do what I *do*—not what I say."[3]

2. Instructing: I Am Doing It Because You Told Me To

Can you remember when your youngster first started to understand your urgent, "No-No!"

Or how good it was when he began to respond to your simple requests, like, "Give the ball to me." And he did just that.

Requests, instructions, directions, explanations—even commands—are an important part of communicating values to your child. But have you ever thought about the tremendous responsibility the Bible's command to children, "Obey your parents," assigns to the parent? If the child is to obey, the parent must give good guidance and worthwhile commands. And he must also make certain the child understands.

And this brings up a crucial point. Many parents overlook or fail to realize that children do not have the ability to understand abstract concepts and values until their late childhood and early adolescent years. Concepts such as love, honesty, respect are only words without meaning for the younger child. Because of this, your child will not necessarily be able to understand fully why you instruct him to do something in a certain way. (His own ideas may even seem more logical!)

Through the years we have taught our children not to fight back if another child strikes them. Instead, we encourage them to talk through differences. Or, if that doesn't work, to be able to say, "If all you want to do is fight, I'm leaving." Now, this doesn't always make sense to the children, but I try to make my instructions

133

clear and let them know that I expect obedience.

Sometimes I am asked, "Are you teaching a value or are you teaching obedience?" My answer is that the young child begins first to identify the values we judge to be important for him by our requiring him to live in obedience to them. The alternative is to avoid teaching the child anything and to wait until he is old enough to understand. Then we can let him choose what he wants to do or not to do.

I believe this latter approach is incredibly naive. Realistically, other adults and the child's peers—not to mention TV—are continually indoctrinating him in the right and the wrong values. And if we wait until he is old enough to understand all the implications, we will have lost the battle. For the most valuable years for building value concepts into our children are the years before they can fully understand cognitively. During these early years, the child needs to be motivated to act in obedience. If the value can be explained and understood, fine. But we cannot wait until the child can understand before we begin to teach.

In my mind there is a basic, biblical value underlying the Christian parent's attitude toward requiring obedience. This value in its ultimate form is obedience to God Himself. He requires obedience of us, His children, whether or not we understand why or even agree with His commands. So it is, as we shape in our children an obedient attitude toward us as parents, we shape their value of an obedient relationship with God.

3. Internalizing: I Am Doing It Because I Want To

The first two value processes—modeling and instructing—logically lead into the third process of internalization. As the child matures and is able to understand more, he is ready to think through the values he has been taught and has identified with. Internalization is taking place as the youngster reaches his own conclusions and makes his own choices.

The concept of internalized values is aptly portrayed in the psalms. Psalm 1 conveys the idea of the person who ponders or meditates on the Word of God. He thinks it through for himself arriving at personal implications and applications. The result? Verse 3 suggests stability and productivity. Psalm 119:11,97-99 also focus upon thoughtful reflection upon Scripture which results in inner-life motivation and conviction.

Parents are also in a key position to guide the maturing child in the process of internalizing values others have presented. Parents can challenge these values, guide their child's interpretation of them and thereby encourage the child's acceptance or rejection of these values.

Helping Your Child to Internalize Values

The key goal for the parent as he teaches Christian values is to guide the child to the point that the young person can act with a sense of Christian integrity and responsibility on his own—independent of his parents. We want our children to be able to act wisely when we are not around. It is when children really internalize standards consistent with the Word of God that their values will flow naturally from proper motives, not just right answers that they "parrot."

Because this process of internalization is so strategic, the parent needs to understand his role in the process. Here are guidelines which will clarify and direct parents in their helping role:

1. Be Sensitive to Value-laden Situations

The alert parent will capitalize on the numerous situations that arise in family life to encourage children to think at a deeper level about values. For example, family discussions related to current events are what I call value-laden. At the time of this writing, much public discussion is related to the integrity of government leaders. What a topic for focusing on personal honesty and responsibility! Hardly a week goes by but what some value-laden event occurs on the national or international scene, at school, in the community and neighborhood. Many of these have the potential to create thoughtful discussion with our children. And we must look at these events and situations against the backdrop of *our* family values.

Events in the lives of family members are valuable sources also for internalizing values. John, age nine, was tempted by a schoolmate to cheat on an exam. He trusted his parents enough to share the event with them. Together John and his parents thought through the implications of honesty and dishonesty. The values of integrity became personalized and internalized for John through this experience.

Another source of value-laden situations is the Scriptures. When the lives of biblical characters are given "flesh and blood," one finds abundant examples of what we are referring to as value-laden. For instance, a particularly important value for family Bible discussions with older children is integral to the story of Joseph and Potiphar's wife (Gen. 39). As a starter you might begin with the question, "Why didn't Joseph give in to Potiphar's wife?"

2. Encourage the Discussion of Values in a Non-threatening, Informal Setting

Recognize the value of stimulating rather than stifling thought. Let's take this situation as an example: Twelve-year-old Ray remarked to his dad, "How do we know that the Bible is the Word of God?" His dad has several possible choices for his response. First, he can list a number of reasons why he believes that the Bible is the Word of God. Or, he can rebuke Ray for doubting. Another possible response would be to invite Ray to examine several Scripture passages and then to discuss Ray's question on the basis of what the Bible says about itself. Obviously, this third option has the most potential for helping Ray think deeply and personally—to internalize this value held by his dad.

So it is essential that parents take time to listen and to respond with wholehearted interest and attention when the child is ready to discuss problems and concerns.

3. Encourage Thoughtful Discussion Rather than "Pat" or Shallow Answers

Under the kind guidance of Christian parents, children should be encouraged to think critically about important life issues. When your child asks, "How come you and mom don't drink beer and stuff like Andy's folks?" compliment him for thinking about such matters and then help him discover meaningful answers in harmony with the Word of God.

4. Discover that Right Actions and Right Attitudes Are More Important than Right Words

One of the common failures of Christian parents (and Sunday School teachers) is to accept the child's words and not probe more deeply to life application. James 1:22 pointedly reminds all Christians to be "doers of the word, and not merely hearers." The clear implication is that the Christian home should be the laboratory of Christian living where the values and ideals of the Christian faith are tested out and found dependable.

5. Recognize and Adopt Those Qualities of Home Life (the Total Home Atmosphere) which Encourage Children to Recognize and to Internalize Wholesome Values

Research has identified the following characteristics in families where individuals developed wholesome values:

a. A spirit of common family participation.
b. Harmonious relationships between family members.
c. Family life with shared confidences and where parents are trusting of their children.
d. Consistent but not severe parental guidance.
e. Positive feelings by child toward parents.[4]

6. Commend Your Child When You Observe Him Demonstrating Healthy Values and Attitudes

At such times encourage your child to do what's right and good by your appropriate comments—such as, "Son, that was kind of you to hold the door for that gentleman." "Marie, I know that it took courage not to hit back in that situation. I'm proud of you." "John, you were right to return the money. God is honored by your honesty." Encourage the child to choose what is right and good by your ready commendation. While we do not want our children to do right merely for the praise of man, we should commend right attitudes and actions.

7. Recognize the Steps a Person Goes Through in Internalizing Values

First, he must be allowed to choose the value as his own. This implies both personal freedom and choosing from options. It is better for our youngsters to learn of

138

alternative views and values under our guidance than be given only one point of view and learn of other options by those outside our family.

Second, the child needs to prize the values he chooses. He should claim the value with a sense of enthusiasm. Prizing a value also includes the idea of telling others outside the family of his choice. In daily living this further suggests another value—that of your children telling others of those Christian values which they believe in and prize.

Third, values become more firmly internalized when the individual has opportunity to act upon them. The more frequently he is able to repeat the action, the more solidly the value becomes his. For example, I desire my children to value the Word of God. I long for them to read it and live by it. However, this value must become their own. When each child has claimed the value freely and acts upon it, it will result in daily reading the Word and obedience to it.

At birth the child is value-less. He identifies with the basic values he experiences in the parent. In early childhood, lacking ability to think values through, we teach him to comply with Christian values as an expression of obedience. During later childhood and adolescence, parents need to focus more strongly upon helping the child think through values he has been taught and claim them for his own.

Integrating the Processes of Modeling, Instructing and Internalizing

Recently I have been particularly aware in our own family of a way that modeling, instruction and internalization are in process as we help our children adopt our value of caring about people, whether they are rich, poor, old, young, Caucasian, Negro, Oriental, or whatever. It has worked in our case like this:

Modeling. During all of our married life we have invited a wide variety of kinds of people into our home. We truly enjoy making them a part of our family. The children have felt and experienced the enjoyment right along with us.

Instructing. We have never allowed the children to use derogatory names in reference to any minority group. We have always encouraged friendships based on respect for the other person—not where he comes from or what he has. We let the children know that ethnic jokes are not all that funny. And we talk through bad attitudes toward others which our children's peer-groups hold.

Internalizing. We stand behind the children when they make a decision. When some of the boys on a ball team wanted to exclude a fellow on the basis of his race, we let our boy know we approved of his efforts to get the black boy on the team. Also, we have helped the internalization process along by asking questions like: "What do you think is right?" "What are you willing to do to show what you believe?" "What is the basis of your decision?" "What does the Bible teach?"

Some who write about teaching values say that the child must be helped to understand the reasoning behind the values being taught. My view is this:

That's fine if the parent can do it. But the most valuable years for building value concepts in our children are years before the child can fully understand cognitively. During these years he must be motivated to act in obedience—until he understands more fully. If the value can be explained: fine, do it. Do not, however, wait to teach values until the child can understand.

It seems to me that there is an underlying value which parents must fully accept as their own and instill it in their young children. This is the value of obeying God—even when we do not understand why He commands us in His Word to do a certain act or hold a certain value. We begin by shaping in our children the attitude of obedience toward us as parents. In this we are shaping obedience and ultimate accountability toward God. And surely this is the value of all values.

Now after our discussion about teaching values—which is another way of saying "building Christian character"—what is the big goal we are aiming for? We have aleady said that we do not want our children's mere adherence to a set of Christian standards or ideals. We certainly want more than slavish conformity expressed in the saying, "If it was good enough for dad or mom, it's good enough for me." We need a deeper basis, a more substantial goal.

The big goal we are aiming for is to guide the child to a point where he can act with a sense of integrity and responsibility—independent of us and independent of other authority figures. The child must be able to act in ways we believe are wise and consistent with our Christian value system when we are not around.

Admittedly, this is a long-range goal, but it is an achievable one if we begin with a specific plan in mind! So we model and instruct the child in order that he or she may act on the basis of internalized standards consistent with the Word of God. And we want these values to flow from honest motives, not just right answers.

PARENTS' PLAN FOR ACTION

The strategic concept that must be grasped in building Christian character is that there are three separate aspects to the process of communicating values to your child: *modeling, instructing,* and *internalizing.* Each aspect of the process is valid, but no one aspect in itself is adequate. Recognize each of the three as legitimate in its own right and use it alone or with another as you deem most effective. Remember also that to some extent all three aspects are valid concurrently, but that each may be more or less important at different times in the child's development.

Where We Are Now

Check appropriate column.   OFTEN SELDOM NEVER

1. We strive to live out the values we consider important in our everyday lives.

2. We attempt to influence our child toward choosing a Christian life-style.

3. We try to make our instructions clear and let our children know we expect obedience.

4. We attempt to be sensitive to those value-laden situations taking place in our family framework.

5. We encourage our children to think critically about important life issues.

6. We make a conscious attempt to guide our maturing child toward independent Christian integrity and responsibility.

What We Want to Do

Discuss the ways you and your husband might integrate the processes of *modeling, instructing* and *internalizing* into your own family framework. Identify the values you feel you are presently transmitting to your child via each of these processes. What are your strong points? Your weak points? How can you improve in each of the three categories?

A good, practical reference that offers fun things for the family to do together at home and teaches Christian values at the same time is Wayne E. Rickerson's *Good Times for Your Family.*[5]

Footnotes

1. Adapted from "Parent's Creed" by Dorothy Law Nolte. Used by permission of the John Philip Company.
2. Erik Erikson, *Childhood and Society* (New York: W.W. Norton, 1963), pp. 247-251.
3. Larry Richards, *You, the Parent* (Chicago: Moody Press, 1974), p. 20.
4. Robert Peck and Robert Havighurst, *Psychology of Character Development* (New York: John Wiley, 1960), p. 106.
5. Wayne E. Rickerson, *Good Times for Your Family* (Glendale: G/L Publications, 1976).